AVAILABLE
ANY BUSH WILL DO

**Remarkable Stories of God at Work
Through Available Lives**

By Doris Ekblad-Olson

First Printing, December 2013
ISBN-10: 0985109289
ISBN-13: 978-0-9851092-8-8

Publication by
ENTRUST SOURCE PUBLISHERS
www.entrustsource.com
Tucson, Arizona

Orders available at www.entrustsourcepublishers.com

All proceeds from sales will be donated to
Evangel Seminary, Hong Kong

First Limited Edition Title:

The Ripple Effect of Committed Lives
as told by Doris Ekblad-Olson

All photos used by permission

The story of Doris Ekblad Olson as told in her own writing in the late summer of 2009
First edition

I wish to dedicate this book to
my dear hubby of 10 years who has encouraged me and
unselfishly released time for me to write it.

To God, who has blessed my life so incredibly,
I submit this for His Glory and blessing to others.

Vern and Doris Ekblad-Olson

CONTENTS

Acknowledgements

The Ripple Effect of Committed Lives was the title of the first limited edition of this second and updated edition of the book. The first edition was produced in 2009 for the McKeesport, Pa. Evangelical Free Church by my faithful prayer partner, Peggy Wein. She compiled the message notes that I had emailed to her of the four talks I had delivered at the Sunday Vesper services at Covenant Retirement Village, Denver, Colorado. They were given in the years 2004 and following.

That first edition came as a total surprise to me. Those talks covered primarily the beginning of my life and missionary journey. It was Peggy's desire to produce and distribute within her church those testimonies to God's faithfulness plus the urging of my friends to write my story that gave birth to this edition. This second edition expands those four talks and adds many more stories of God's incredible faithfulness using a number of weak but available vessels.

I have used English names for most Chinese individuals in these stories but not necessarily the English names they chose. The stories are random samples of what I have seen God do in both my life and in the lives of others, proving that "Any Bush Will Do." Space and time limit me because I am going blind. I am writing now with limited peripheral vision only. This makes this work an extra challenge—for His glory.

In my forty-four years of missionary service in Hong Kong and since, I've repeatedly seen God produce fruit that remains. He has worked in remarkably unpredictable ways by using various lives that were available to Him. My childhood and youth experiences are included here to show how early God begins to mold a very earthen vessel for His use. Never underestimate God's work in the hearts of small children.

For this edition, I owe special thanks to my editor, Margaret Shickley, whose untiring encouragement and hours of work has made this book possible. Since encroaching blindness has made it extremely difficult for me to even see what I have touch-typed, you may realize the enormous significance of her contribution to this book.

I am grateful to a number of Covenant Village residents for their help in proofreading a chapter here or there, to Marion Sustad who proofread most of the chapters, and especially to Daryle Ann Hise for her expertise with the final proofreading of the whole book. Other residents here have contributed by reading back to me parts of my writing to help me catch duplication and errors.

I am grateful to retired missionaries, John and Arlene Nelson who unrelentingly pushed me to write this story.

Last but not least, I am indebted to my techie friend, Debra Carlson, whose technical skills kept my computer running and adapted to my low vision.

Most of all, thanks to God for so blessing me through the years that it would have been amiss for me not to share it by this book.

May this brief testimony bring God glory and motivate you to become more AVAILABLE to Him!

I wish here to recommend another book (of 100 pages). It is the biography of my father's unusual life and pioneer ministry in the early 1900's in Inner Mongolia, North China. Before his death in 1972, Dad tape recorded much of his remarkable story. His granddaughter, Joy Mielke, transcribed his first person testimony for his biography, "AN ORDINARY MAN -- A GREAT GOD" and self- published it in 2011.

To round out the record of my father's life, she freely copied verbatim parts of my childhood story as told earlier in the first edition of this book. So expect some repetition of my story in her book.

I highly recommend her book, available on many web sites, as a unique story in the history of missions. It should be in every Christian home to inspire a vision for missions. My story is simply a continuation of my father's. In fact, although he passed away in 1972, you can still hear his voice today relating bits of his personal testimony to God's faithfulness on the following web site: AgreatGod.com.

Introduction

We are familiar with the story of God speaking to Moses in the desert through a burning bush. But WHY did God choose to use THAT particular bush to speak through? Was it especially beautiful? Fragrant? Magical? No. There was nothing special about that bush except it was simply there. AVAILABLE! So God used it. Clearly, ANY bush there would have done!

We don't focus on that bush but on what God did THROUGH it. Today we gaze in wonder when we see God work in remarkable ways using weak human vessels. Don't focus on the vessel. Remember, "Any bush will do."

I need not pray for God to use me. That's up to Him. My part is simply to bow in humble submission before Him, my sovereign Lord. I pray that my life will please and glorify Him like Jesus who said "I do always those things that please my Father." I long to be a burning bush available for God to use anytime and anywhere; and, then be alert to where He is already working and join Him in it. We can choose to daily make ourselves available to God. "Good morning, Lord. What do you have up your sleeve today? Count me in on it. I'm AVAILABLE!" Then we will see Him work, in us, through us, around us and for us, beyond expectation.

Chapter 1

MONGOLIA THROUGH A CHILD'S EYES

(Based on a Talk Given at Vespers in 2004 at Covenant Retirement Village of Colorado)

I'm happy to share with you some of God's blessings in my childhood as a missionary kid in Mongolia! You seldom hear of the impact of missions on a missionary kid. That's what you'll get now. Our scripture is from the 86th Psalm.

Psalm 86:8-12

8. "Among the gods there is none like you, O Lord; no deeds can compare with yours.
9. All the nations you have made will come and worship before you, O Lord; they will bring glory to your name.
10. For you are great and do marvelous deeds; you alone are God.
11. Teach me your way, O LORD, and I will walk in your truth; give me an undivided heart, that I may fear your name.
12. I will praise you, O Lord my God, with all my heart; I will glorify your name forever. "

BACKGROUND

As my childhood memories allow, I hope to share with you some reflections of a rather unusual kind of life in far-off Inner Mongolia. It is my hope that you will carry away with you the deep impression as the Psalmist says in 86:10. *"God, you are great and do marvelous deeds; you alone are God."*

I want to focus here on childhood memories of Mongolia. First, I must clarify that I spent only 3 childhood years in Mongolia—from age 3 (1933) to age 6 (1936). Still, they left me with many indelible memories.

HERITAGE

My father, Knute Hjalmar Ekblad, was born in 1889. Although raised in Sweden, he came to the United States before his 18th birthday. Here he lived with a Swedish Christian family in Chicago, worked with them at a book bindery and went with them to the Summerdale Evangelical Free Church. He saw Jesus in their lives. One night after a church service, old man Jackobson was so full of the joy of the Lord as he was putting away the folding chairs, he burst into spontaneous song. That simple act struck home to my dad. "How can any man be that happy?" He went home, knelt by his bed and trusted Jesus as his Savior and Lord.

When he offered himself to God as available for anything, anywhere, he felt a burden and call to China. Friends agreed that must be so for he even LOOKED

Chinese! (His Chinese appearance was to be a real advantage in his future ministry.) For preparation, Dad was educated at Moody Bible Institute, Bethel College, Garret Biblical Institute and Chicago Theological Seminary.

He returned to Sweden where he was commissioned by the Swedish Alliance Mission (Svenska Alliance Mishoon). From Sweden he took the Trans-Siberian train across Russian Siberia to North China, traveling by rail, rolling across Siberia, sitting 18 days and nights on hard wooden benches all the way to Vladivostok on the coast of China. It was the last train to get through Siberia before the 1917 Russian revolution! Dad's age then was twenty eight. Next he headed back inland to his ultimate destination where his mission had work in a part of North China called Inner Mongolia (Outer Mongolia to the North was at that time ruled by Russia). Chinese filled the cities of Inner Mongolia while the Mongols lived up north on the grasslands. Dad's ministry was to be largely among the Chinese. Dad was like that burning bush, simply available. Now, what would God do through this available Swedish "burning bush" in far off China?

Dad's diary, written in Swedish, tells of language study and street meetings where he preached daily, often 3 or 4 times a day, to gathered crowds. Often he traveled by bike or horseback to outlying villages to preach to first time hearers. Eventually, after several years, he married Alma, a fellow missionary. Baby

Harold was born to them a year after their "China" wedding.

Day after day, Dad enthusiastically shared the Gospel to curious crowds. He was refreshed as he returned home to his beloved little family, wife Alma and baby Harold. Little did he realize how severely the Enemy would attack and seek to knock him off the mission field. Then see how available he would be!

ENEMY'S ATTACKS

About a year after Harold was born, Alma gave birth to seven-month, premature twin girls. With only limited medical help available, one twin died at birth; but the other little preemie was kept alive for three months with hot water bottles in lieu of an incubator. Sadly, pneumonia still claimed her short life. Dad had to make a second small coffin to bury this twin, also, in the Martyr Cemetery for missionaries and missionary children. This cemetery existed from the days of the Boxer Rebellion of the early 1900's when so many missionaries in China were martyred.

But, little Harold continued to thrive and bring the Ekblads much comfort and joy as they grieved the loss of their twins. At eighteen months of age, Harold was a ray of sunshine. He was such a happy boy, just learning to walk and talk. But, some well-meaning new missionaries, unaware of the danger, gave him some local food from the market to eat. Little Harold got sick, developing diarrhea, then dysentery. No good medical help was available. Dad had led to Christ a Chinese doctor who had also studied some Western medicine. He pumped the baby's stomach and battled for Harold's life but to no avail. Precious Baby Harold, also, went home to be with Jesus. Dad told how he and Alma laid little Harold in a cardboard box and sat with him that warm summer evening in the moonlight of their walled-in yard. There they wept and prayed together. They thanked God for the eighteen months that they'd been allowed to have him and for all the joy he'd brought into their lives. Now a third little coffin was laid to rest beside the twin girls in that Martyr Cemetery!

Just a few months following, Dad was out in some outlying villages for meetings when a messenger came with the news that his wife Alma was very sick. Perhaps her immune system was down from the recent grief. Dad hurried home to find her delirious and in a coma with typhus fever. There was no chance to say good-bye. She never regained consciousness. Just seven days after contracting typhus fever, she passed away also. The finality of it! Dad's whole family wiped out! His grief was overwhelming. That was his fourth and final family member to be buried that year in the Martyr Cemetery. Was he still available to God?

EMOTIONAL HEALING

By this time, Dad had already stayed his seven year term on the field. After all the grief he had endured, fellow missionaries urged him to take a break and return to the United States for furlough and healing. Dad later stated that when he returned by ship after that extra-long term and the loss of all his family, he felt so lonely. "All the world seemed to me like a great wilderness, and I was the only one in it, but I had Jesus." He got a cabin on board ship with a room to himself where he could weep and pray and sing, praising God. Upon arrival in Seattle he picked up a newspaper that reported how a man who had just lost his wife committed suicide from grief. Dad thanked God that he still had Jesus for comfort so he could go on.

On that furlough Dad shared in the United States his burden for China. He spoke in many churches and to the China prayer band at Moody Bible Institute. There at a prayer meeting for China, he met my mother, Selma Nelson, who was a Moody student headed for China. She, too, was available to God. Although they became engaged that furlough year, Dad did not wait for her to finish school before he returned to his ministry in Inner Mongolia. There were so many people there who had never heard of Jesus.

After her graduation from Moody, my mother, Selma Nelson, followed him to Inner Mongolia. However, their mission station was the property of the China Inland Mission. The C.I.M. had a requirement that each new missionary must be on the field a minimum of two years before getting married. This was so they could focus on learning the Chinese language. Finally, in 1925, my parents were married in a simple ceremony there on the mission compound. My mother's diary states that the Chinese who lived and worked with them on that station did not realize there was anything between them until the day of their simple wedding.

Eventually, another set of twin girls were born prematurely. Life was very primitive and medical help was scarce. Although one twin was stillborn, the other twin, little Esther, gave them much hope and joy; but after just three weeks of life, she turned blue in my mom's arms. My mother frantically massaged her to restore circulation but Baby Esther died in her arms. Probably the baby's heart was not fully developed. Within a month my dad had to make two more little coffins, now his 6th grave in that Martyr Cemetery. In my mother's diary I read, "The Lord gave and the Lord took away. Blessed be the name of the Lord".

REGAINING CITIZENSHIP

Since my dad had overstayed his first term in China and was a naturalized U. S. citizen from Sweden, he discovered upon his first return to the United States that he had lost his U. S. citizenship. Fortunately, he had dual American and Swedish passports so he was able to return to China as a Swede after that first furlough. But in 1926-1927, political unrest in China forced my folks out of China and home to the United States for an extended furlough. During this time, Dad decided to remain in the United States for five years to regain his U. S. citizenship. By this time my brother Paul and I were born, while Dad pastored first the Wyanett Evangelical Free Church near Cambridge, Minnesota, and then the Trade River Evangelical Free Church in Wisconsin, nine miles south of Grantsburg. Out of Dad's seven children, only two of us "made in USA" survived.

EARLY TRADE RIVER MEMORIES

I have memories of life in our Trade River parsonage before I was three years old. Our fenced-in yard was on a bluff above the highway. My brother, sixteen months older than I, knew how to open the fence gate. One day I promptly stepped out, lost my footing and rolled down that steep bank to the highway below. In my mind's eye I can still see that gravel highway and hear my brother calling for my parents. Thankfully, I was not run over that day as God had other plans for that little tyke.

The Trade River General Store was just beyond our church. That store had everything from food to clothes, shoes, boots, saddles, grain, seed, sleds and miscellaneous farm hardware. Of special interest to my brother and me were the toys in a back room of the store. The store-keeper's twin kids, our age, used to bring those toys out to the cemetery between the parsonage and the church, where we kids would play with them among the tombstones. I marvel today at the freedom our parents gave us, just three and four years old! When we returned from China three years later, we ran to that back room of the store and, sure enough, those used toys were still there!

TRIP BY SHIP

In the summer of 1933 my folks began preparations for the trip back to the Inner Mongolia area of North China. The day before we were to take the train from St. Paul to Seattle, my brother Paul, then age 4, fell and broke his arm. It seemed the Enemy was determined to derail us. But as a family we proceeded, anyway, with Paul's arm in a cast. Still available to God?

As we waited on board ship in the Seattle harbor, I remember looking down at the black water, asking why it wasn't blue. My brother wisely answered "It will get blue when we get farther out." I was three and he was four. I remember the raised edge around the ship's dining tables to keep the dishes from sliding off when the ship pitched in troubled waters. A short chain anchored each table and longer chains held our chairs from sliding too far when the ship tipped. I also remember myself and my chair sliding away from the table, my food in my lap and my being terribly seasick. The trip to China by freighter took a full month.

TRIP INLAND

I don't remember the 3-day train trip inland from the China coast to our city of Kwei Wha, the capital city of Inner Mongolia at that time; but I have painful memories of that first ride by oxcart "taxi" from the train to our mission station. I cried because my head banged repeatedly against the wooden vertical bars of the tarp-covered cart. This was the traditional means of travel in our city but I never got used to it. Those covered carts pulled by mules, donkeys or oxen had no springs and the roads were rough with deep ruts. In rainy weather when the ruts were filled with water, a large rock hidden under the water would almost tip the cart over as the wooden wheel climbed over the rock.

OUR HOME AND CHURCH IN CHINA

In the United States you have a yard around your house. In China our house was built around the yard. A string of rooms and walls surrounded a courtyard. We lived in the inner compound where we had a small vegetable garden with a brick walkway around it. There was a well where we got our water by a bucket and windlass, like the wishing wells in this country. All our drinking water had to be boiled. Around our well where water had spilled, there was luxuriant grass—a novelty in our city. Most yards and streets were packed mud, faithfully swept daily with bunches of branches and then sprinkled with water to settle the dust. All the grass in those yards had previously been pulled up by the roots and boiled for food in times of famine. On washdays our washing machine was pushed out to the well. Because we had no electricity, the agitator was powered by pushing and pulling a hand-held lever on the side of the machine.

Attached to our inner compound by a small gate was a larger compound where Chinese Christians lived who worked for the mission. At times the outer compound also housed refugees and Bible School students. It had a barn for our cow, some goats, chickens and the main gate which was our only exit to the street. Our gatekeeper and family lived beside the big gate. Our church was located between the inner and outer compounds. The church had packed dirt floor, rough benches, and a pot-bellied stove in the middle which was no match for the Siberian winter winds. The men sat on one side of the church and the women on the other. Along one wall were windows—rice paper windows.

The overflow crowds and those too shy to enter the church would wet their finger, touch the paper, and leave a hole with, eventually, a lineup of eyes on the outside. They could see in; but we couldn't see them. Eventually they got brave and came inside. Those paper windows were replaced every week.

Many believed the Gospel and were baptized. I remember one man who came to our services whose face had the sallow drawn look of an opium addict. He was so gloriously saved that his appearance changed dramatically. He just beamed with the joy of the Lord. I called him "the man with the shining face". Eventually he had to leave our area for a season and we did not see him for some time. When he returned, I took one look at him and ran crying to my parents saying, "The man with the shining face. His face has lost its shine!" He had backslidden and fallen into opium use again.

KIDS LEARN CHINESE

Upon our arrival to our mission station, I remember the Chinese children running up to us children and talking in a strange language. It was a local dialect, a very off-brand of Mandarin, which my folks already knew. We'd ask our folks what the children said and asked how to answer them. We then got the Chinese kids from the outer compound to come to our door. We'd run inside, repeat what they'd said for our folks to interpret and ask how to answer them. I remember that very soon we didn't need to ask our folks to interpret. We did all our play in Chinese. Only to our parents did we speak English. Children both learn and forget a language quickly. Fortunately upon our return to the United States in 1936, my brother and I totally forgot this off-brand dialect. Otherwise, it would have been harder for me to learn proper Mandarin sixty years later in 1996, just before my retirement, for my anticipated work in the United States with Chinese students. In Hong Kong we spoke Cantonese.

OUR PLAY

Our parents explained to us that our toys must last seven years until our furlough. If they broke, they could not be replaced. We carefully put them back on the shelf each night before bedtime. Some of them were made of celluloid and did break easily. I had two dolls named Big Nice Doll and Little Nice Doll. A wicker doll buggy brought from America got crushed in shipment and I was crushed over it. Dad saved the wheels and metal frame and for Christmas gave me a new buggy that he had locally made of varnished wood. I was thrilled. I used it mainly to haul around the endless number of puppies from our watchdog.

A favorite game that our Chinese playmates played with us was a guessing game. The small group of kids would sit on the steps to our living room. The kid who was "It" would face the rest, holding out two fists and ask each child "In which fist is the stone?" After each guess, the kid who was "It" could turn his back and switch the stone to the other hand. The first kid to guess right got to be "It". We did not need expensive toys. I have happy memories of those play times with my Chinese friends.

When I was five, someone sent to us from the United States a children's two wheel bicycle with training wheels. My dad put it all together and I could hardly wait for my turn to try it. My brother was quite sickly. Even with the training wheels, my folks supported him on both sides on his first short ride. When my turn came, to the surprise of all, I just took off, riding fast naturally, without instructions, with the training wheels turned up. I screamed "how do I stop?" Dad said, "Run into the wall" which I did at full speed and landed in a heap. Ever since and through all my years in Hong Kong, a bicycle has been my means of transportation wherever possible.

SECURITY

For security we had two large watchdogs which were chained by day. After people had gone to bed at night and the main gate to the street closed, the dogs were let loose to roam around the compound to scare off robbers and intruders. China was noted for its thieves and robbers. The dogs developed fierce temperaments. Once in the daytime when Dad wasn't home, one of the dogs got loose. It was chasing Chinese children in the outer compound who ran screaming. My mom watched through our window petrified and didn't know what to do. I snuck through several rooms and exited to the courtyard so Mom wouldn't see me. I went straight to that fierce dog unafraid. Those watch dogs were nobody's pets; but, since I loved their puppies, I had no fear. The dog, recognizing my fearlessness, followed me meekly to be chained again. Looking toward the living room window, I saw the look of horror on my mom's face as she saw me lead that fierce dog back to its doghouse!

OUR FOOD

Sz Sz Foo was our cook who also went to market to buy our food. We ate the staple food of North China. It was millet. (In this country you use millet for bird food!) It was understood that only rich people in South China could afford rice. We ate millet in some form three times a day – millet porridge, millet noodles, and millet dumplings. I hated the sameness of millet. We had a whole drum of millet standing in our kitchen. I would kick that drum when no one was looking. Really we were very fortunate. Every day hungry beggars came to our big gate. They were never turned away. My folks never gave them money; but there was always a pot of millet porridge on the kitchen stove so every beggar received a bowl of hot gruel.

Mom was very nutrition-conscious and raised all the vegetables that she could in our little garden and canned them. My folks didn't trust the local meat which was covered with flies as it hung in the market. All the meat that we ate, my dad hunted in the mountains, just seven miles outside our city. He would bring home roe deer, argyle sheep, mountain goats or pheasants. This is where Chinese pheasants originally came from. I remember crying over a colorful pheasant rooster that

Dad brought home, because I thought it was too beautiful to die. Mom canned the meat so we could eat for some time from each hunting trip. Dad was often gone out to villages for evangelism. We had dessert once a day only when Dad was home; so we always gave him an especially warm welcome home! (He never knew why!) Dessert was generally precious imported canned fruit. I remember one Christmas when Dad brought us a gift of a bag of some local peanut candy. It was also a memorable day when we received a box of chocolates from friends in America. We spaced them out to last a lo-o-o-n-ng time.

We remembered eating ice cream in America so we asked Mom what it was made of. "Sugar, eggs and milk" she told us. Well, we had a cow and chickens and sugar; so why not make some? "No ice cream churn," she answered; but one day a truck loaded with furniture, driven by Caucasian government people, drove into our yard. Of course, we kids asked if they had an ice cream churn among their furniture. They answered, "Yes, and it's packed on top so it's not hard to reach." We ran to Mom with the great news. "Now we can have ice cream!" Her answer! "No ice". It was a hot summer day and we had no electricity. The lady, who came with the truck, asked us kids, "Why don't you pray for some ice". She was no doubt mocking us; but we took her seriously and went into the bedroom. I remember kneeling by the bed praying for some ice while the ice cream churn was there. We went back out and told the grownups that there'd be ice soon because we had talked to God about it! I expect that the government lady was embarrassed. However, that afternoon the weather turned hot and muggy and a storm blew up. In the three years I was there, this was the only time I know of that it hailed. The hailstones were as large as strawberries. My mom swept up a bucket full, placed it around inside of that wooden ice cream churn, added salt on the ice to make it colder, and we had ice cream that one time, a direct answer to the prayer of faith by two kids.

COPING WITH WEATHER

Dad had the hides of the animals that he hunted tanned and made into warm winter garments for us. With the fur turned inside, we wore these indoors and outdoors in the winter time. The winters were intensely cruel. The poor little Chinese children ran around in padded garments with split bottom pants instead of wearing diapers. I wondered how they could stand the cold. Their homes were almost entirely one big raised brick platform on which the whole family slept and ate, plus a walkway beside the platform. A metal door opened alongside the side of the platform for burning sticks, dried cow dung or coal. So they practically lived all winter on top of this brick fireplace called a "kang".

Their homes had no bathing facilities and water was scarce so they had no baths in the winter. Body lice and fleas were present everywhere. Dad said, "When they sing at home in their mission meetings of the millions over there, I'm tempted to think of something else!" Chinese people would sit along the street chewing the hems of their padded garments to kill as many lice and fleas as possible which gathered there. In our home we had a washtub for Saturday night baths. Every night Mom would check us kids over for lice and fleas.

A very few times an airplane flew over our city and we would all run out to see it. My dad made the comment, "Some people say that someday missionaries will travel by plane, but that could never be." When I asked him why, he answered, "It takes a month on board ship to get rid of your lice and fleas. You don't want to bring them with you back to America, do you?"

It seldom snowed; but I do remember once when it did. We had great fun rolling snow into a snowman. Instead of snowstorms, we had dreaded dust or sand storms sweeping down from the Gobi Desert and shutting out the sun so that it grew dark. Although we tried to stuff rags into all the cracks around the doors and windows, the sand still entered. There was a layer of sand over everything in the house. It got into our hair and even ground between our teeth.

The Chinese wore mostly cloth shoes; but we ordered our shoes from Montgomery Ward. First, Dad would put his foot on a sheet of white paper and draw around it. Then Mom put her foot inside his outline and drew hers. Then my brother and I did the same. We sent that sheet of paper to "Monkey Ward" and asked them to send us each a pair of shoes to fit each outline. They did.

HEATHEN SUFFERING

I have childhood memories of two kinds of suffering resulting from heathen customs and beliefs. The Chinese believed the girls' feet must be bound from the time they were six to eight years old or they would never get a husband when they grew up. Each night I'd hear the little girls screaming as their feet were bent with the toes under the foot and tied tightly. Eventually the foot stopped growing and it could fit into a tiny shoe. They would actually walk on the tops of their feet. After this painful process each evening, the girls would sit screaming in pain with their feet hanging out the window. The window sill would cut off circulation making the foot fall asleep and relieve their pain. You could always recognize an adult woman at a distance if she was walking. They walked with arms outstretched for balance on their tiny feet.

Another night sound was the sound of loud wailing by women who had just lost a child or loved one. They put a cloth over their head to hide their face and simply let out their pent up grief. They had no hope of ever meeting their loved one again. Their loud wailing carried far in the still night air. Don't tell me the heathen are happy with their religious way of life!

SPIRITUAL IMPRESSIONS

I have no memory of children's meetings or a Sunday School for kids; but in our home our parents were careful to keep God central. Every night either Mom or Dad would tuck us into bed, tell us a Bible story and pray with us. Every morning after breakfast, we'd have family worship together. If Dad was home, he'd lead; otherwise, Mom would read from the Bible and we'd have prayer together. She explained to us that both our parents had dedicated each child to God before we were born. Our parents told God that they didn't want any of their children in hell. If this baby wouldn't grow up to love and follow Him, then take him to heaven while he is a baby because babies go to heaven. That was real child dedication. After having prayed that way, Mom said, they could never complain when God took five of their little ones to heaven because they'd rather have them there than in hell. I got the message when I was very young that only a life lived for God was worth living.

We kids couldn't figure out why our folks would come to a land so far away that our aunts and uncles and families couldn't come to visit us and to a place with no ice cream. Our parents always answered, "We came to tell people about Jesus"; but we couldn't connect that with the Old Testament bedtime stories of Moses in the bulrushes and Daniel in the lions' den and our coming to Mongolia. One morning after breakfast devotions, when Dad had gone to a village, we began asking Mom questions, trying to make connections. She said, "You children are so young. From the questions you ask, I think you are ready to hear the whole story; but I have appointments this morning. Tonight put your toys away extra early and I will put it all together for you." We were so excited that day that we could hardly wait.

That night I wasn't very happy with what I heard. I remember that Mom said we all had to choose whether we wanted to belong to God's family or the devil's family. I was scared of the devil; but I thought that if I chose God's family, I'd have to be good for the rest of my life. No way! I was born naughty and I knew it. For me, to be really good one whole day and not to scrap with my brother seemed an impossible mountain to climb. I could never make it. I had my first conviction of sin. I was four years old. I had never seen nor heard my folks scrap. It must be easy for grownups to be good, but not me, a little kid. I decided I would become God's child when I grew up; but for now, it was impossible. Somehow I missed the truth that in becoming God's child, He would change me on the INSIDE! After Mom put us to bed, my brother asked me, "What did you decide?" I answered, "If God wants me, He can come and get me". That put the responsibility upon God. I was so gloating over my clever answer that I forgot to ask my brother about his decision.

TO THE GRASSLANDS

Dad used to travel through our city gates to outlying villages by bicycle or by horseback. Then, unexpectedly, he got a 1927 Chevy touring car from a wealthy American lady who had wanted to spend her last retirement years in a Buddhist monastery. Needing a car to get there, she had a 1927 Chevy touring car shipped across the Pacific. Quickly disenchanted by the monastery filth, lack of water, bathing facilities or heat, she returned to America. This lady sold her car to Dad for very little because it would have been too expensive to ship it back to the United States.

Since there were only 2 cars in our whole province, there were no gas stations! Dad had to arrange to buy gas shipped in 5 gallon cans by rail from the coast and then carry five gallon cans of gas and water in the car when traveling. Roads outside the city were practically non-existent. Dad drove down dried river beds or over the mountains where we had to stop to roll away rocks to get through and add water to the radiator when it boiled over. However, the car certainly facilitated getting the Gospel to the outlying villages. When our car had breakdowns, Dad had it towed back to the city by oxen, donkeys or camels and he had to figure out how to fix it himself.

With our car we brought supplies to TEAM missionary friends, the Stuart Gunzels, who lived on the grasslands where they worked among the Mongols. (Dad worked to reach the Chinese.) There were plenty of poisonous snakes on those barren grasslands. Our folks taught us kids to stand still if we saw a snake and wait until it was gone before we moved again. That trick probably save our lives more than once.

On one trip to the grasslands, we had to set up camp for the night at the foot of the mountains. While Dad scouted around looking for something edible for supper, my mom spotted a large jack rabbit. Dad's gun was still dismantled in a case in the back seat of the car because it was required by law in the city. Mom put the gun together and shot the rabbit for supper. Dad was so proud of her.

Dad pitched our family tent for the night, digging a shallow trench around it to keep us dry in case of rain. Tent flaps were up to allow for breeze. Just the mosquito netting hung down. That night in my sleep I rolled into the trench and awoke to see the moon and stars through the netting and hear the wolves howling nearby. My terrified cries aroused the whole family.

My best girlfriend on the grasslands was a little Mongol girl named Kong Ker. I don't know how we communicated because we didn't speak the same language. In one visit there she was so excited to see me and not knowing how to communicate, she put two fingers up my nose and I got a nosebleed! When on the grasslands we always stayed in a Mongolian yurt. The yurt was made with a portable frame and was covered with felt wool made of camel hair which was quite wind proof.

One day, unknown to my parents, Kong Ker's family took my brother and me to a Mongolian devil's dance at a large stadium. The dancers, with huge animal head masks, danced before them. The people sat in terror because at the end of the ceremony someone from the audience would be chosen for a human sacrifice. Fortunately, we left before that part and obviously, I was not chosen. Older missionaries warned our family never to visit a devil's dance because the missionaries who had gone there had never come back!

VILLAGE TRIP

On one very memorable village trip we went as a family together over mountainous terrain. I was carsick and whining. Dad assured me that we would go no farther than the Chinese village in the valley below us. Upon arrival, Dad pulled a tarp over the car so villagers wouldn't mess with it. Mom and Dad played their mandolin and violin and the whole village gathered around. My brother had very blue eyes and snow white hair, common to Swedish children. The Chinese believed that blue eyes meant you were blind and white hair meant that you were old. My brother's looks helped to draw a crowd. We ran off to play nearby with the kids while my Dad spoke to the grown-ups. It was common for missionaries to ask how many had ever heard of heaven and hell. Oh yes, they all knew about heaven but they had no hope of ever getting there. They were just doing pious deeds, burning incense and sacrificing to idols in order to get lighter punishment in hell. My dad told them that God made heaven for them and provided a way for them to get there. That was news to them; so he told of Jesus' death on the cross to pay for our sins and to reconcile us sinners to God. One of them asked if they could get their ancestors out of hell now and into heaven. Dad explained that this decision must be made while we're still living. One of them asked how long we had known about this. "All our life", Dad answered. "Then why didn't you come sooner to tell us so our ancestors could have heard?"

MISSIONARY CALL

We stayed overnight in that village, ate their food and slept on their "kang" or hard brick platform bed. In the morning they asked my Dad to tell that story of Jesus again. One of the village leaders asked my dad if we couldn't just stay in their village to teach them more about this because they had never heard it before. However, Dad had appointments and a heavy schedule. He couldn't stay. He hadn't expected this village to be so ripe for the Gospel. Don't think that the heathen are any more eager to change their religion than your next door neighbors are. Prayer partners had been praying for spiritually hungry hearts and this resulted in this village being so ripe to receive the Gospel. The village leader then asked, "If you can't stay here with us to teach us more, could you send a teacher to help us?" I was playing alongside and saw my dad hang his head. In sorrow he replied, "I'm so sorry. I have no one to send you." I felt so bad that these folks wanted so much to hear but there was no one to send to tell them. In my heart I told God that I knew I wasn't his child yet; but I would be when I grew up. If He wanted me to, I'd be glad to return to tell the Chinese about God. I kept this to myself because I feared my parents would treat this as a childish idea. To me it was a solemn commitment between a five year old child and God. I could never get away from this commitment. Again, never underestimate what God can do in the heart of a child.

MOM'S HOME GOING

We returned to our city, home and church. Winter came and people struggled for warmth. Easter Sunday was in March that year of 1936. We had a lively Easter service with much singing. The pot-bellied stove and many bodies helped to warm the church in spite of its paper windows. Mom played her mandolin at that service like she was inspired; but she caught a cold that day and was frail in health. After getting out of bed on Monday morning, she collapsed and couldn't speak. Dad helped to get her back in bed and went to try to find a doctor of Western medicine. Dad got a missionary doctor to come the next day with his small black bag of medicines. The doctor said, "I think it is meningitis. She needs to rest." The doctor could do nothing more. That night Dad and we kids knelt by her bed and prayed. Dad begged God to heal her. When it occurred to Dad that God might heal her by taking her to heaven, he prayed, "If you must take her, take us as a family all together. How can I care for these two children with my work scattered all over?" Finally Dad prayed, "God, I trust you. Your will be done." In the morning when we woke up, Dad explained, "Mommy has gone to be with Jesus!" My first thought was my words. I had said, "If God wants me, He can come and get me." I thought I had made a bargain with God and He had taken me up on my bargain. He didn't get me because I wasn't ready. He took my mom instead. That's how I understood it.

Dad had to leave us kids to go out into the street to buy boards to make his seventh family coffin. Local coffins were hewn out of hollow logs. Since this was the seventh grave for our immediate family, Dad had plenty of experience making coffins. The Chinese Christian ladies covered the coffin with black cloth and helped my brother and me to make paper ringlets out of colored construction paper in lieu of flowers. There were no funeral homes out there and no florist shops. The burial had to be the same day. The ground in the Martyr cemetery was so frozen that the men had difficulty digging the grave. Several missionary ladies from nearby heard the news and made it to the grave side funeral service with the weeping Chinese Christians. Dad preached the funeral service. We kids sat in the car for the grave side service to keep from catching cold. Dad had fought his battle the night before; now he was comforting the Chinese Christians.

SALVATION PRAYER

When we got back to our mission compound, I realized that I'd never hear my mother's voice again. Dad had to type a Swedish letter to inform family and friends back home of Mom's home going. Dad did not dare to send a telegram because it would be too cruel to telegraph the news and keep them waiting three months for a sea mail letter giving the details of how she died. That night Dad asked my brother and me whether we were ready to go where Mommy was. We both knew we weren't. That night we both asked Jesus to forgive our sins and we gave our lives to Him. We wanted to make sure we would see Mom again. God could correct our motives later.

TOUGH DECISION

Dad knew that he couldn't care for us and still fulfill his mission work. (I remember on that first morning after Mom died that he put my shoes on the wrong foot!) What would Dad do with two small children? Fortunately, that had been settled months before. My mom knew before she left the States that if she went back to Mongolia, she would never return. God had revealed that to her. Mom said her final goodbyes to her best friends before leaving the States; but this did not keep her from going. She was still available to God's leading. I remember one day at mealtime when she said to my dad "I know I won't be going back to America with you and the children. I wonder what you plan to do with the children when I'm gone." Dad didn't want to hear what she said; but she said that she'd feel more comfortable if they'd discuss it. "What would you want me to do?" Dad asked. Mom said that she'd like her sister in St. Paul to care for the children. So when Mom died so suddenly and was unable to speak, Dad knew what to do.

ORPHANAGE EXPERIENCE

While he booked and waited for a ship for us to go first to Japan and then another ship for America, Dad made arrangements for us to stay a couple of months in a neighboring city with a missionary couple, Philip and Matillda Anderson, who ran an orphanage. We actually stayed with Auntie Mat and Uncle Philip in their home next to the orphanage; but we played often with the orphanage children. Years later on a return visit to a church in Inner Mongolia, I met one of those playmates, now an eighty year old woman, who remembered our play times together at that orphanage.

HEAD FOR JAPAN

Dad took us with him from inland China to the China coast and then to a ship for Japan. Freighters made stops along the way to load cargo. At one such stop Dad left the ship to go ashore to buy us some bananas as a parting gift for his precious children. When the ship's loading was completed, the gong sounded for the ship to pull out, the gangplank was pulled up and Dad was not back. Although we knew the captain's quarters were off limits, we children ran crying to the Captain begging him to hold the ship until our daddy got back. To our relief Dad came running up on shore with the bananas. They let the gangplank down for him to board and we were happily reunited.

PARTING WITH DAD

At the last stop in Japan Dad explained, "I'm sorry I can't go back with you to the States. There aren't enough people here to tell the Chinese about Jesus. I've written instructions to the ship captain and the sailors to transfer you both to a train for St. Paul when your ship reaches the United States. Jesus will take care of you". This was a six-week ocean voyage. My brother was seven and I had just turned six. My brother had also been very sickly. Once Paul asked my folks "Will there be flies in heaven?" When he was assured no, he said, "Oh, that's good because I don't have the strength to chase the flies off my face". He was that weak. Dad had little hope of ever seeing my brother Paul again. Perhaps that was the hardest part for Dad in sending us kids off to America while he continued his work in North China. This was a heavy price that he paid to be available as God led him. During that separation, Dad cherished the words in Revelation *"There shall be no more sea"*. The sea separated him from his children!

In my heart I knew Dad loved us. Dad staying behind just underscored for me the urgency to tell the Chinese of Jesus. I said to myself, "You don't know it now, Daddy, but some day I'm coming back to help you". God used that as part of my call to the mission field. Dad stayed with us on board ship a few days while the freighter ship docked and loaded in the Japanese harbor. Dad got us settled into the on-board routine and showed us parts of the ship where it would be too dangerous for us to go, because there was no net around the railing to catch us if the ship lurched. Dad showed us how to go to the dining room when the gong sounded for meals. We kids had bunk beds in our tiny cabin. Paul's comfort was a small night light on the wall beside his pillow. My comfort was the small ladder to climb to the upper bunk. On that final night, our first night alone, Dad had to leave the ship and sleep on shore because the ship was scheduled to pull out at 4:00 a.m. the next morning. Due to heavy fog, that departure time was uncertain. That uncertainty made the separation a little easier. Maybe we would see Dad again the next morning! The fog horn kept sounding throughout the night; but at 4:00 a.m., the ship pulled out to open ocean. I still have difficulty sleeping past four a.m.

VOYAGE TO AMERICA

We soon became known on board ship as the two little kids who didn't belong to anyone. However, God in His providence proved that Jesus did care for us. Sometime on that trip a single missionary lady on board, "Auntie Susie", a total stranger, heard of us, took us into her cabin and cared for us the rest of the trip across the Pacific, transferred us to a train and accompanied us all the way to my aunt's home in St. Paul. There we had a glorious welcome by crowds of friends and news reporters who met our train. We were showered by a bewildering number of gifts – new toys! It was almost too much for us to handle all at once. My Aunt Hilma wisely hid most of them, rotating them periodically so we would not be overwhelmed.

Our story became national headline news – two small children crossing the ocean alone. Friends have sent us some newspaper clippings that they had saved of that story with our pictures. The news reporters failed to mention how Jesus HAD cared for us by Auntie Susie.

TWO YEARS AT AUNT HILMA'S

We had loving care for two years at my Aunt Hilma Swanson's home in St. Paul, Minnesota. Since I had lost both home and parents, it meant so much to me that she would sit in her rocking chair with me in her lap, rocking and singing hymns to me. I felt loved. At that time my aunt was not a professing Christian; but she had a beautiful voice and sang hymns all day as she went about her housework.

An example of my aunt's kindness was the time we got our first ice cream cones of our life, strawberry and chocolate. We were all dressed for a party and it was a very hot day. My brother wisely instructed me that since it was cone shaped, we should bite the end of the cone and suck it out. We could not keep up with the melting ice cream. It was all over our clothes. When my aunt came out to get us, she never scolded but forgave us. She took us inside, cleaned us up and redressed us for the party. This incident always reminds me of 1 John 1:9 which tells us that *God is faithful to not only to forgive us our sins but to cleanse us from all unrighteousness*. Aunt Hilma did both.

My seven year old brother had other "wise" observations like the reason our folks didn't want us to look in the mirror too much was because we might wear it out. One day he told me he had figured out how to fly. He said, "I haven't tried it yet but I know it will work. You take one jump in the air and before you come down, you take a second jump and then another and then another and pretty soon you are flying". I was jealous that he had thought of it first. When I went out behind the house and tried it, I couldn't believe how fast I came down and that I could never take that second jump (but it did work wonderfully in my dreams). When I told my brother it didn't work, he said dejectedly

"Yeh, I know. I tried it too." That method
to fly was as ineffective as people who try to reach God
by their own good works and spiritual effort. It
doesn't work.

My Aunt Hilma's husband, Uncle John, was a
kind baker. We fell in love with their dog named Pal,
too. The Swansons had a Model A Ford which Uncle
John cranked to start. He would drive us to our maternal
grandparent's home in North Branch (Kost), Minnesota,
where my mother grew up in the Kost Evangelical Free
Church.

The St. Paul Payne Avenue Evangelical Free
Church was just three long blocks away from the
Swanson home. Aunt Hilma did not attend church; but
she sent us walking to Sunday School and church every
Sunday. I was deeply gripped by my Sunday School
teacher, Dorothy Swanson, telling the story of the
Apostle Paul's shipwreck. Probably it was our own
recent ocean voyage that contributed to that fascination.

I remember my first day at that large St. Paul
public elementary school. I expected to be able to read
after my first day of school and I couldn't wait to read. I
stopped off at the local library on my way home where I
checked out a third grade book. That evening I laid
down on my tummy on the kitchen floor; and with
determination I spelled my way through that whole
book while my aunt cooked supper and patiently
pronounced every word that I spelled out. I marvel as I
recall her patience and my persistence. Because we
were a bit late starting school, we managed to complete

grades one through three in our two years living with Aunt Hilma.

My brother and I would catch ourselves naturally talking to each other in Chinese as we played. People would stop and stare in surprise at this so we determined to stop it. Stop it we did. When our dad came back to the United States two years later, we had lost it all. By then Dad's Chinese language sounded as strange to us as to any American kid.

DAD AND THE JAPANESE WAR

My father stayed on in North China until his furlough time came in 1938. During those two years, the Japanese war began. News came out in the St. Paul newspapers that our dad was missing and presumed dead in North China. (He had just gone to the mountains to hunt for meat.) It was a painful, false report. The Japanese war was against China, not yet with the U.S. Still, several times the Japanese soldiers nearly took my dad's life. God wonderfully protected him! However, those two years were a time of great spiritual harvest in China. Furthermore, Dad and our mission station there were instrumental in saving the lives of many refugees. Many of whom were also transformed by the Gospel.

Before Dad returned to us in the States, he had remarried a Swedish-speaking, Finnish, Salvation Army missionary serving in Mongolia. So we were able to have a home again as a family. Our step mother had studied just enough English to be able to learn Chinese from English text books. We heard a lot of Swedish in our home after she came.

DOOR TO CHINA CLOSED

After the Japanese war and the Communist take-over of China, Dad was never able to return again to the Mongolian part of North China. Not a speck of news from North China came through to us in the United States for over 50 years. Dad longed to hear whether the church over there had survived the war and persecution. Little did I realize that it would take 46 years before I could get back to our old home in Inner Mongolia where I could again see the Christians that I left behind as a child in 1936. I wanted to know if any "fruit" remained of my parents' service. Had their sacrifice been worth it? Was anything left of their ministry? I would not know this until 1982 when I made my first trip back to Inner Mongolia. What I found was beyond belief. If only my folks could have seen ahead one half century the "fruit" of their labors. I discovered an incredible spiritual harvest. It was the spiritual fruit of lives who remained available to God regardless of cost; but that is another story!

God has promised and proven that His word will never return void! Our God is a great God, doing marvelous deeds, far beyond expectation! He alone is God!

Chapter 2

UN-ORTHODOX MISSIONARY BEGINNINGS

(Based on notes for my Second Vespers talk at Covenant Retirement Village)

Psalms 57: 7b-8, 10-11

7. I will sing and make music.
8. Awake, my soul! Awake, harp and lyre! I will awaken the dawn.
10. For great is your love, reaching to the heavens; your faithfulness reaches to the skies.
11. Be exalted, O God, above the heavens; Let your glory be over all the earth.

I t has been my great privilege to praise my Lord among the nations, and how I long to see His glory over all the earth!

Actually, there is a story behind every life. Life stories that are very different from our own hold a special interest. So I would treasure the opportunity to hear YOUR life story too, which will certainly be very different from mine! I especially like to hear how God has worked in your life; how He has brought YOU to Himself, to sing and make music because you have experienced His love and faithfulness.

Really, missions begins with the work of God in the heart—often years before one ever gets to a mission field; so I will fill in a bit about those early years long before I ever went out as a missionary myself. They impacted my life and world view.

TRADE RIVER, WISCONSIN

When Dad returned from North China in 1938 with a stepmother for us, our family moved from St. Paul to about 75 miles north of there, just inside the Wisconsin border. Thirteen miles of Jack Pine Woods lay between us and the St. Croix River which separated Wisconsin from Minnesota. We lived in a tiny two room house in Trade River, Wisconsin (Unincorporated) about ten miles south of Grantsburg. (If you look on a map, you'll see it is sort of the end of the world. Beyond that for miles there are no towns, just wild life refuges that are wild and beautiful!) Trade River, Wisconsin is where Dad had been pastor before we went to North China in 1933 and Trade River has been home to our family ever since.

My brother and I lived with our stepmother in that tiny two-room house (plus an outhouse) for one year while Dad traveled to do deputation for the mission. The year that I was nine was a year for plenty of adjustments. To us kids, it was adjusting to a stepmother who was just going through menopause and always crying. She had never been in the United States before, had little idea how to handle two squirming children and spoke only broken English which she had to learn in order to learn Chinese out of English textbooks. She was a Swedish Finn. It was a hard year for all of us; but things got better.

IN MAPLE RIDGE, TWO YEARS

Since Dad couldn't return to North China due to the Japanese occupation and then the Communist takeover, he was offered pastorates in the Twin Cities. His burden was always for the small country churches struggling financially to continue. The depression was still on. He figured that, since he had learned to live on so little on the mission field, he could probably survive where most Americans couldn't. Thus he hoped to help some small churches and prevent them from closing.

Dad accepted the challenge of a call to a small Evangelical Free Church in Maple Ridge, Minnesota just across the St. Croix River from Trade River. That church could only afford a pastor's salary of $25.00 a month. Our parsonage had kerosene lamps instead of electricity. We heated and cooked with wood and had running water only when we ran out to the pump to pump it! Farmers would at times drop off potatoes, eggs, butter, and other farm products to help us out. Dad got some turkey chicks and a few goats, which was my job to milk, and we had a big garden. Mom canned much of its produce. We never went hungry and I never thought of us as being poor; although looking back, I remember I had just one secondhand skirt and sweater to wear to school my whole first winter. I was satisfied with that. I identified with my folks' world view which saw living on little as an exciting creative challenge! Years later that became significant in my own missionary experience. In fact, I even look back with nostalgia on those two years that we lived like pioneers as Dad served that loving little Maple Ridge country church.

Mom did her ironing at church because they had electricity there, and I'd go with her. While she ironed, I practiced preaching as I pounded the church pulpit. I was about ten.

During the two years that we lived in Maple Ridge, we kids attended all church services with our folks whenever the church doors were open. Dad's messages made a deep impression on me spiritually. I could hardly wait to get home after Sunday morning services to gulp down my dinner, get my ukulele and head out behind the barn to the stack of sweet smelling fresh oat straw. There I would sit against that straw pile all afternoon, singing Gospel songs, accompanied by my ukulele, until the joy of the Lord overflowed into tears rolling down my cheeks. No one but God ever saw or heard that child experiencing God by that straw pile.

NORTH SCHOOL

Because my life had already been uprooted several times, my experience at this new school was anything but happy. However, it became spiritually significant to me. That first year in Maple Ridge Paul and I attended the "North school" which was a two-room country school for all eight grades. Our room had grades five through eight. Although my brother was a year and a half older than I, we were both in grade five.

Our teacher, Miss Johnson, made learning fun for her pupils by making one student the "dunce" who would stand up front before the whole room while she encouraged the other five or six classmates to attack that dunce with rapid-fire math questions. This would cause the dunce to get too rattled to respond. It was a fun game for the whole room, fun for all but the dunce! I, as the youngest and the most vulnerable in the room, was the teacher's chosen "dunce" and I was attacked this way daily. Today it would be called "abuse"; but God turned it eventually into blessing for me.

The teacher picked on me daily, mercilessly. She managed to convince both me and the rest of the pupils that I was stupid and without normal intelligence. It took some years for me to overcome that self-image which could have kept me from ever getting to the mission field.

To avoid the painful present, I escaped into story land by devouring nearly every book in our small school library. However, I found it difficult to focus or concentrate to write up the required ten book reports. Even some reports that I did finish, Miss Johnson admitted to losing so she made me redo them. I

sometimes cried before heading for school in
the mornings.

My other escape from the painful abuse was to
daydream of more pleasant things. My thoughts would
drift to the stories I'd read, to our farm or to the animals
that I loved: the goats, turkeys, cats, other animals and
the endless adventures available there.

But there was a price to pay for daydreaming.
Many times a day, Miss Johnson would announce
before the whole room "Doris, get busy! Quit
daydreaming". Miss Johnson usually kept me after
school to make up for the time lost by daydreaming.
Thus, I would have to walk the three miles home alone.
In the winter it got quite dark before I arrived home; but
God was with me and I became a survivor. I enjoyed the
lonely walk home by singing memorized verses of
Gospel songs as I walked. I felt God was very close to
me on those walks. It became the high point of my day.
I sometimes took a shortcut through a cow pasture; but
there was a bull in that pasture and I remember running
for a hollow tree to hide in until he left. I prayed and
God protected me. He turned abuse into blessing. As I
walked those miles, the words of the hymns ministered
to my childish heart. Actually, tears of joy welled up
overflowing down that ten-year-old's cheeks. Even
children can experience God's presence.

Many years later when I was home on furlough
from Hong Kong, I was given Miss Johnson's phone
number and I called her. By then she was elderly and
frail but she remembered me. She asked what I had

been doing with my life. I couldn't resist answering casually that I had been teaching for years in the Orient on the college level: English, Greek and Hebrew - in Chinese! All God's grace! He could even use a dunce! (I still don't know the multiplication tables.)

SOUTH SCHOOL

During our second year in Maple Ridge, Minnesota, we attended a different elementary school. No doubt that might be quite different from your experience. It was a one-room country school with one teacher for all eight grades but not all grades had a student. That school really welcomed my brother and me because we brought the student body to a total of ten kids. If less than ten, they would have had to consolidate! Our teacher, Miss Wright, was exceptionally kind and encouraging.

One wintry Monday morning, it began snowing just at the start of our school day. It snowed heavily all day and became too dangerous for us to hike the mile and a half home after school; instead, our whole school, all ten of us bundled up and held hands while the farmer from across the road, who came for his second grade daughter, led us kids, plus Miss Wright bringing up the rear through the blinding snow to his farm house. The whole school holed up there for three days until the storm was over. The phone lines were down so there was no way to contact our parents!

On Wednesday afternoon we tried to make it home because it had stopped snowing, the sky cleared and the wind had blown the road clear in front of our school. When we made a right turn toward home, that road, which cut through rolling hills, was blown level with snow. We sank in soft snow up to our arm pits. Walking through such deep snow was laborious. Paul, who had always been weak and sickly, wanted to stop and rest. I feared that if he did, he'd fall asleep and never make it home.

A grown man came by on skis and saw our desperate plight. We still had over a mile to go. He was not too far from his own farm and being a strong man, he figured he could make it home without his skis; so he loaned us his pair of skis. We took turns skiing a short way and then scooted the skis back to the other until we reached home. He really saved our lives. We arrived home well after dark that Wednesday night to the great relief of our parents. I had to soak my frost- bitten feet in cold water. God spared our lives with no more serious effect than frost bite. We were snowed in for two weeks before the rotary snow plows cleared the roads for school to start again.

OUR ANIMAL FARM

Once while still living in Maple Ridge, Dad bought an additional nanny goat, "Fanny." Our other goats were mean to her so she went with our landlord's cows through the pasture out to the woods. At milking time I went searching for Fanny. I felt sorry for her because she was rejected by our goats. Although I called for

Fanny, she and the cows had gone too far into the woods where I went searching. Suddenly I realized that the sun was setting and it was quickly getting dark. Already too far from home to make it back before dark, I began looking for a place to spend the summer night. I picked a spot under some white pine trees with a thick layer of pine needles; then I heard my Dad's voice in the distance calling for me. Up to this point, I felt sorry only for Fanny. I felt calm and collected as I picked my spot for the night like I had read in my brother's Boy Scout books. At the sound of Dad's voice, I ran crying to him screaming at the top of my lungs, "Daa-dyee!" Guess I was not so brave after all.

For a time we had a very stinky Billy goat. Someone borrowed him to mate their nanny goats. They brought him back in disgust, saying he jumped up on their car and his feet pierced through the canvas roof of their car! Also, when the farmer's wife had her wash hanging on the line, the Billy goat ate a hole in nearly every pair of long johns on the line. We soon got rid of him. Otherwise, I enjoyed our animals. Every morning and evening it was my job to milk our nanny goats. Such was life at our home, school and church in Maple Ridge, Minnesota.

TURKEY SERMONS

Two turkey stories that remain in my memory are worth sharing. The first occurred during the two years we lived in Maple Ridge, Minnesota when we raised a small number of turkeys. One hen successfully hatched out 23 chicks. She was a good mother, caring fervently for her chicks, teaching them to eat, drink and follow her to lush feeding spots for a balanced diet.

One day when the chicks were just a few weeks old, we noticed that Mama hen's comb was turning dark. This meant she had contracted black-head, a contagious and terminal turkey disease. She must be separated from her chicks and the other turkeys or they, too, would die. What would become of her chicks? We isolated the Mama hen to a corner of the goat barn, by a few horizontal jack-pine poles. That evening her chicks gathered outside the goat barn, crying pitifully because they missed their Mama. Under whose wings would they sleep that night? How could we comfort and protect them?

Surprise! Remarkably, big old Grandpa Gobbler, heavy though he was, managed to scale the goat barn threshold and head straight for Mama Hen. He stuck his head between the horizontal poles and seemed to communicate with the sick mama hen, getting her how-to instructions. Then he returned to the chicks, clucking to them just like Mama Hen used to do. They crawled over and under him while he spread his large wings to shelter them.

In the morning, Grandpa Gobbler struggled again to scale the high goat barn's threshold, reported briefly to Mama Hen and then led the whole brood on a day's feeding journey. All twenty three chicks followed him through the alfalfa field, through the harvested field of oat stubble that was swarming with grass hoppers and through the cow pasture in the evening on their way home, filling up on its short grass for dessert. Again he reported to Mama Hen and another night he sheltered the chicks as though they were his own. This continued a few days until Grandpa Gobbler saw Mama Hen lying dead in the goat barn. From then on he raised those chicks alone to adulthood with a caring fervor equal to any mother hen. What does this tell us about the love and care of our God for us? A God who could express His heartfelt care for us through the example of a turkey! "Under His wings my soul shall abide, safely abide forever". (Song: <u>Under His Wings</u> composed by Ira D. Sankey and written by William O. Cushing)

Another turkey story is not so beautiful. After moving to our own farm in Trade River, Wisconsin, in the early spring we would order several hundred turkey chicks from the hatchery. Each turkey chick had to be taught to drink and eat finely ground feed. They were a lot of work. As they grew older, they were kept fenced in an area with fresh grass. When the grass was gone, they were moved to another newly fenced area of fresh grass. It took our entire family to surround and direct the flock from the old site to the new one. Close to Thanksgiving time, they would have nightmares at night that resulted in a screech sending the whole flock flying in every direction. Some folk were happy to have a grown turkey land in their yard around Thanksgiving time. We had to hunt for them, round them up and drive them toward home. One hen was particularly naughty. She wanted to dash off in another direction from where we were steering them. Other turkeys would follow her.

I learned to identify her among the other hens, and saw this trait in her repeatedly. When she did this, she set a bad example for the other birds and it frustrated our efforts to give them new grass.

One day after she had done this several times, my temper flared up at her. In chasing her back, I gave her a kick. Then she limped! I wanted to cry. I felt so bad that my anger had caused this poor, dumb and helpless bird pain. She could no longer move fast or lead the others astray; but I hurt for her and felt so ashamed. Nor did I want my family to notice her limp and ask why. Since walking was now painful for her and I felt so sorry for her, I picked her up and carried her that day and whenever we moved the flock. She liked being carried and petted, so she would come to me to be carried. She became our "tame hen". Only I knew why she was so tame. Although her limp did not last, she remained a constant reminder to me of my temper for which I still had to deal.

God spoke to me through that turkey. Dashing off and going my own rebellious way, contrary to what I knew God wanted, would also bring painful consequences. I did not want to be a rebellious stubborn turkey. Yet I knew I had a loving heavenly Father who would pick me up, comfort and care for me if I went my stubborn way with its painful consequences.

THE CHALLENGES OF FARMING

Dad had always dreamed of living on a farm. "If I had a farm, I could support myself and help other small churches like this one." A banker, back in Grantsburg, Wisconsin, who knew Dad, contacted him. "We have so many bankrupt farms on our hands that we don't know what to do with them. I'll make you an offer. You can have this 80 acre farm in Trade River if you'll just sign for it. We know you and trust that you will pay us when you can!"

So we moved to this Trade River, Wisconsin farm where the former owner, although an experienced farmer, had gone bankrupt. Dad was 50 years old and had no farming experience. He had never farmed a day in his life and had no farm equipment. Our farm was surrounded by clay-soil farms but our farm was a sand farm and very dependent on rain. It bordered on Little Homes Lake that was continually restocked with fish by Trade River coursing through it. One neighbor farmer told my dad, "Yeah, you got a sand hill beside a slough hole". Dad loved to fish. He pulled a lot of fish out of that little slough hole; and, eventually, supported a number of mission projects from that sand hill.

BLESSING FARM

Dad had the audacity to call our 80 acre farm, which was part swamp, part lake and very hilly, "Blessing Farm". The house was more than 70 years old and made of huge logs, ten to twelve inches in diameter. The logs were fastened together with wooden pegs. The logs were not a tight fit; so light and wind came through between the logs. The roof leaked; but, by faith, it was to us "Blessing Farm".

In fact when our few belongings were moved by truck from Minnesota to Blessing Farm, Dad had the trucker wait before unloading the furniture. "First we are going to dedicate this farm to God. We are going to farm for missions. If God blesses, we will fix the roof as soon as possible so we won't have to come home from church to put the pans out to catch the leaks. We're not going to buy fancy furniture." Our furniture was just old garage sale and auction stuff. Dad said, "We want it understood as a family that together we are going to farm for missions." After Dad's prayer to dedicate the farm to God, the trucker then could unload the furniture. Those were Dad's priorities. Dad insulated the house the Chinese way. He plastered the cracks between the logs with soft, fresh cow manure! I objected, "Daddy that will stink." "No," he said. "I've learned from the Chinese that when it is dry there will be no smell; instead it will be excellent insulation." He was right. It was cool in summer and warm in winter. The walls indoors were finished with wall board and colorful wallpaper so no one knew the secret of our cozy home. The outside he had covered with siding. In time our roof got fixed and even our antique furniture grew into value! It was indeed a blessed farm.

A HUNDREDFOLD RETURN

While farming, Dad did continue to pastor the Maple Ridge Evangelical Free Church until that church could eventually afford to support their own fulltime pastor. With Dad's farming and God's blessing that little country church not only survived but it grew until the church had to be completely remodeled by adding a full basement and other additions. The Maple Ridge Church lay across the St. Croix River, only 40 miles from our farm as a crow flies but much farther by road. In the summer a small river ferry with a car motor and a paddle wheel could take one car at a time, a half hour trip, across the river. In the winter the St. Croix River would freeze over. At times when the ice was thin, Dad had the nerve to give the car the gas and cross with the ice cracking loudly behind him! We'd be so relieved when he made it home safely, especially in the dark, after Sunday night services. Little did my dad know that the little country church he saved from closing would one day help to support his daughter on the mission field for 44 years! *Eccl. 11:1 "Cast your bread upon the waters and it will return to you a hundredfold."*

HOLY COW!

When we first moved to the farm, Dad had just enough money to buy one heifer who gave us her first calf—a bull calf. Neighbors taught Dad that to get the best value from a bull calf he should let it suck all of its mother's milk for six weeks and then sell it for veal. So he did. We drank powdered skim milk ourselves. Dad's sister, his brother and wife from Chicago asked to come to stay at our farm for a week. Dad sighed and said, "I wish I had money to buy real milk for my guests. They're well-to-do city folk. They'd never understand why we drink powdered skim milk." On the day our guests arrived, a Guernsey cow appeared in our pasture.

We phoned neighbors far and near but no one had Guernsey cows or knew anyone who did. It would either have had to walk a long distance down the road, where surely it would have been seen, or come through many fences, cross many fields and finally get to our pasture. We checked our fences. No problem there. Where had it come from? It was a mystery. By evening the cow was uncomfortable with so much milk. So I milked her each morning and evening for a full week. On the day our guests left, that cow disappeared! To this day we don't know where she came from or where she went! Simply God's creative provision! A Holy Cow! Over and over I saw God do incredible things. I was learning that I could trust Him. This was practical missionary training.

MULTIPLIED BLESSINGS

Dad knew nothing about farming but neighbor farmers were glad to give advice. Dad would exchange labor by working three days in exchange for a farmer with horses and equipment helping him one day. So dad had no control over when our farm work got done. He had to wait until the other farmers had time to finish their work before they could help him. There were no hay crushers in those days to speed the drying process; so after he got the hay cut, we needed at least three sunny days with low humidity and no rain before we could take in the hay. Otherwise, rain would wash out the hay's color, taste, vitamins and value. Neighbor farmers had to get their own hay in before they had time to come to help Dad. More than once I saw the dark clouds come when Dad's hay was dry and just ready to take in. When a few large drops of rain began to fall, Dad would say out loud, "Well, Lord, that will be less money for missions" and I saw the rain stop! Neighbors noticed and it became a byword in our community, "Watch when Ekblad has his hay cut, and then cut your hay. God doesn't let it rain on his hay!" The blessing of God! We were farming for missions and God was blessing! I saw many examples of this.

I remember once when we had a whole seven acre field of oats cut and ready to be shocked so the rain would run off. Dark clouds came rolling in. My Dad and we kids worked furiously to shock it all before the rain. We had just finished the last shock when the clouds burst forth a downpour. We kids ran for cover; but Dad knelt right there in the field, in gratitude, thanking God. I guess he was so wet with sweat that the rain didn't matter. Those were some of the priorities that I grew up observing. They were missionary beginnings for me.

LOSING A RING IN A HAY STACK

In haying season, we worked together as a family, pitching hay onto the hay wrack, pulled by a Ford Ferguson tractor. Dad would then stack the hay right, so rain would run off. One winter, we had more than enough hay, so Dad sold one haystack to a neighboring farmer, Conley Peterson. Together Dad and Conley reduced that stack by pitching load after load onto Conley's hay wrack, which he then hauled home.

After the haystack was nearly gone, Conley discovered that his wedding ring was missing! How could they find a ring in a haystack? Four inches of fresh snow covered the surrounding ground. Dad said, "A wedding ring has special significance. I believe God would want us to find that ring". With pitch forks in hand, the two farmers bowed their heads and prayed for help to find that ring.

Just then Mom called from the house, TELEPHONE! " Dad ran home for the call on that bright, sunny day. On his way back to the haystack, Dad's peripheral vision caught sight of a gleam of the sun's reflection in the snow, not far from the haystack. It was the wedding ring! It was sunk below the snow's surface, visible only at that exact angle, visible to a man very legally blind but available to God. Two farmers again bowed together to thank and praise God. Oh, what a God we serve!

NAVAJO OUTREACH

One summer a neighbor farmer hired a group of American Navajo Indians to come and cut pulp in his woods. They came with their families and swarms of kids to live in makeshift shacks that they built in the woods for temporary quarters. Each shack had mostly one big bed on which the entire family slept. Neighboring farmers felt them to be a threat. They feared that their chickens would disappear. The truant officer repeatedly tried to find those children hiding in the woods to get them to our little one room country school but it was a losing battle. Obviously, they would never come to our church either. My young heart was burdened to reach them for Christ. I was overjoyed when our pastor suggested that our church string band could go to those woods every Friday evening to sing and play for the Indians; then, he would give a devotional to introduce them to Jesus. We did this every week that summer but I could see we were not making progress. We were just an amusing diversion for them. The message didn't sink in. They lived close to nature. I decided they must see a miracle in nature to convince them that our God was real. I imagined a week when it would rain all week, day and night, including on Friday. On Friday evening we would go to the Indians with our instruments and umbrellas; then Pastor would announce to them that we were going to pray to our God in heaven and ask Him to stop the rain for our service. If they would see that happen, they would believe.

One week it did rain like that all week. I was so excited with anticipation. Here was our chance to show the Indians that our God is real. I could hardly wait that Friday for our 8:00 p.m. string band service for the Indians. That afternoon our pastor called to cancel the string band service for that evening due to the rain. I nearly cried. I suggested to the pastor that it would be a wonderful chance to go there and pray for the rain to stop and then the Indians would believe when they saw our God's power. The pastor cleared his throat in embarrassment at this childish proposal. "Well, I've already called quite a few to cancel tonight. We'll meet again and play for them next Friday night." I hung up in tears. I then prayed, "God, if it was O.K. to go to them and pray for the rain to stop, would you do this just for me? Make it rain up to 8:00 this evening and make it stop right then."

At this time we had quite a few cows. I went to the barn to milk them that evening, finishing about 7:30. It was still raining. But, as our grandfather clock struck eight, the clouds parted and the setting sun shone through. Every leaf and blade of grass sparkled with drops of water in the sunlight like jewels in a magic fairyland. I cried with joy because I knew then that it was O.K. for me to pray like that. I asked God to help me when I grew up to remember this and to keep a simple faith in His power. Help me not to get mixed up like grownups. I grew up seeing and expecting God's miracles.

OUR HOUSE ON FIRE

After we had lived for five years on the farm and gradually improved it, our cozy log house burned down on September 2, 1945. I was just fifteen. It happened the weekend before the start of my junior year of high school.

That forenoon we had a chimney fire in the chimney of our new kitchen addition. It burned out the accumulated pine tar in our chimney. A good thing! But, upstairs the chimney stopper in my room got over-heated from the chimney fire and must have dropped sparks to the floor boards below which slowly smoldered.

Normally, after lunch, I would have been taking an afternoon nap in that room; but my brother and I were raising cucumbers for a nearby pickle factory. We decided that afternoon to pick "cukes" instead. A strong hot wind was blowing. From our cucumber patch, we heard our stepmother yelling for Dad who was out in a field cutting hay with our new Ford Ferguson tractor. Hearing her, we commented, "How does she expect Dad to hear her above the noise of the wind and the tractor?" When we looked toward the house, we saw smoke and flames pouring out through the roof. Mom was standing on the front steps waving her apron up and down and yelling for Dad.

We both ran. Paul ran for the house and the phone to ring the long emergency ring that called for help from both neighbors and the town fire station that was nine miles away. One long ring contacted all twenty-some parties on our phone line. I ran for our car and drove out to the field for Dad, honking all the way. Cars began to arrive. Neighbors began running in and out of our house to help us rescue what valuables we could. In the confusion, I found myself carrying out a pitcher of milk! Very quickly, the flames got too hot to even get close.

By that fall, Dad had added a kitchen to the house plus a half-basement underneath for a pump with water pipes to the barn for the cows. Our stepmother had canned all our harvest from that summer's gardens. Those jars of canned goods stood in neat rows on shelves in that basement under the new kitchen. They held all our fruit and vegetables for the coming year. We did not have money to buy food in those days. We raised and canned what we would eat for future months.

SUMMER CANNING SAVED

Because heat generally rises, the basement was not yet as hot as upstairs. When one burning wall of the kitchen fell outward, it exposed the basement shelves with all those jars of food. To lose all that summer's harvest besides the hours spent growing and canning it would be added pain.

One neighbor, who responded to the emergency ring on the phone, came with two strong German war prisoners entrusted to him as farm hands. When those Germans prisoners looked through the missing wall and hole in the floor to see those jars of food on the shelves in the basement, they couldn't stand it. They voluntarily took more risk than anyone else.

Wearing heavy leather gloves, one of them jumped down into the basement with the house burning above him. He began tossing those jars up to his buddy who passed them on. Instantly a bucket brigade formed of neighbors passing those hot jars down the line to set in the grass under trees in the yard far from the house. It got so hot down in the basement that some of the rubber jar rings had begun melting around the edge. (We ate those jars' contents first.)

After the last jar of food had been brought up, that German prisoner was pulled out of danger just in time. At considerable personal risk, those heroic Germans plus our neighbors saved us a year of food. We will always remember them for it.

The fire truck from town arrived much too late to help. It quickly ran out of water. When refilling the tank from the river, sand clogged the hose nozzle. We could only stand helplessly as we watched our home burn. It was a heart wrenching experience for this teen-ager. I was devastated. Where was God in all this?

SAFE AM I

Dad was standing apart to one side. I snuck up behind him and heard him softly singing the song, "Safe am I, safe am I, in the hollow of His hand. No ill can harm me, no foe alarm me, for He keeps both day and night. Safe am I, safe am I, in the hollow of His hand." (Chorus: <u>Safe Am I</u> written and composed by Mildred Leightner Dillon) Although we had lost virtually everything, Dad's faith in God was strong. This was extremely reassuring to me as I stood there hand in hand with Dad, watching our home and belongings burn.

Dad had debated whether buying fire insurance was a lack of trust in God; so he let his fire insurance payment lapse. His insurance company sent him a second notice to say that he was past the deadline. If he paid up immediately, his coverage would continue. At the time of the fire, Dad couldn't remember whether or not he had sent the payment. Fortunately he had. This, at least, gave him the benefit of $2,000.00. After this experience, he never again questioned the wisdom of buying fire insurance!

The out-buildings on our farm all lay in a roughly North-South line. The house was farthest South. The strong hot wind that day came from the North West. If the wind had turned much, all our out buildings would also have burned. My brother's beehives that sat on blocks south of the house got hot enough to blister the hive's exterior paint; but inside the bees, by fanning their wings, kept the temperature even so the wax combs did not melt!

The flames continued burning those huge logs for a week. After the fire, we kids slept at our neighbors; but our folks slept in the granary oat bin on a sheet over the soft oats with the granary doors open to watch if the wind would change. One night the wind did turn to send hot embers blowing toward them and the granary. Instead of running, they just knelt in the oats and prayed. The wind promptly returned to Northwest and held there for that entire week as the fire continued burning. PTL!

Three weeks after the fire, I went down in our burned out kitchen basement to try to identify melted objects like the glob of aluminum that had been our large pressure cooker. A large sturdy steamer trunk from China had been somewhat protected so it didn't burn. I opened it and immediately the contents burst into flames. I slammed the lid down but it was too late. With oxygen now it all burned. It had stayed that hot for three weeks after the fire. That trunk was filled with photos and snap shots from China. Irreplaceable loss!

REBUILDING MIRACLES

Our September 2, 1945 fire happened during the war when building materials were as scarce as hen's teeth. The series of miracles involved with our house getting rebuilt so we could move in on Christmas Eve were enough to cause one of our two carpenters to become a Christian.

Our neighbor carpenters were too busy to come and help us rebuild until early November, two months after the fire. Dad asked them to cover the new half-basement under the kitchen first to protect the water pipes to the barn for the cattle. Dad had long before sawed up lumber and stacked it in his wood lot to dry, intending to eventually build a chicken coop. What a blessing! That wood was now dry and available.

November brought unseasonably mild weather, so Dad told the carpenters, "Go ahead, put up some 2 x 4's for the ground floor and see how far we get." One evening the carpenters came to Dad saying, "Now, Ekblad, you must decide where you want your rooms and doors and windows downstairs." It was a one night decision. Soon they came with the same request for the upstairs rooms and stairs. Again it was decided in one night. God led marvelously for the future use of that house for ministry hospitality.

A good neighbor insisted that dad build a full basement under the rest of the house too. He volunteered his own time, his team of horses and an earth-scoop to make that a reality.

Dad had only enough lumber siding for part of the house. Due to the war, there was none available in any lumber yard he contacted. The carpenters said the work must stop because they could do no more without it. That night at our church weekly prayer meeting, Dad gave this as a special prayer request. A farmer came to prayer meeting that night that never came otherwise and did not even attend church regularly. After the meeting, he told my dad that he had some lumber cut and stacked in his pasture. Maybe Dad could use it. It was just enough to finish the siding on the house.

Dad could find no flooring available anywhere for our kitchen, entry way and bathroom. One carpenter asked Dad, "Didn't you used to have a wooden silo before this concrete one?" Dad said yes. It had blown down so he stored the wood in the barn. It was beautiful fir wood and just enough for our need.

The bricks needed for the new chimney were also unavailable anywhere! Freezing weather was coming and bricks could not be laid if the weather was freezing. Another neighbor told Dad, "I have a pile of bricks behind my barn from when I wanted to build a hen house and the fire insurance company did not allow it. I don't know how many but you're welcomed to them if you can use them." It was enough for all but 3 bricks found elsewhere. They had a fire burning at the ground level of the chimney to keep their hands and the concrete warm enough to lay those bricks all the way to the top before freezing temperature came.

There were other miracles, too, in finding needed doors and windows available that were just the right size. No long joists were found for the roof; so they had to go with shorter joists, spliced at an angle for a "gambrel roof". This was a blessing that provided four upstairs bedrooms with squared off rooms with the slant only in the full length closets. That special roof provided room for a hospitality ministry for traveling missionaries who often stayed with us. Years later my brother raised his four children there. Many times we thanked God for the blessings that came through that fire and for our lessons that we learned through it.

These are just a few samples of God's blessing that enabled us to rebuild that house and move in on Christmas Eve! I witnessed the fact over and over that God is worthy of our trust.

THE PULL OF THE FARM

I loved that farm and claimed it half way to China. I remembered my feeling when we were on the ship returning from Mongolia as a kid, having lost my mother, father and home. I had felt like a cork floating on top of the ocean, tossed by the waves in every direction, and wishing I could sink to the bottom and anchor somewhere. Now at last our farm was paid for. We owned it. We were there together to stay. I was anchored at last, firmly to that farm! We worked the farm together as a family and I loved it, animals and all.

FISH STORIES

Some mornings Dad would come and wake me at five a.m. "Let's go down and get some fish for breakfast." The creak of the oars on a still morning as we steered our rowboat quietly down the river to the lake with the sunrise mirrored in the water is a treasured memory. We both loved to fish. Those delightful days made me want never to leave the farm. Our stepmother was not one to work well with others; so I didn't learn housework or cooking. Mostly, I did outdoor work with Dad and loved it.

Macular degeneration runs in our family. My dad lost his central vision long before he lost his yen to fish. Although he could see neither his fish line nor his cork, he used his peripheral vision to fish. He'd throw his line out to the side of his boat while staring straight ahead. He used a long, white chicken wing feather stuck into his cork that would move to signal when there was a bite. Thus, he continued to pull in sunfish, perch, crappies and bass to grace our table.

MY OWN GARDEN

For example, Dad gave my brother and me each a patch of garden, side by side, where we could plant anything we wished. When company came, Dad would surely ask them, "Wouldn't you like to see the children's gardens?" Of course, what could they say? So Paul and

I competed for the most prolific weed-free garden. We both became lifetime avid gardeners. I hoped to marry a farmer and raise a dozen kids on a Wisconsin sand farm and make it work. Those were my dreams; but I'd always remember, "I'm so sorry, I have no one to send you" and I knew in my heart that someday I must leave the farm and go to China as a missionary.

BOTTLED MESSAGES

In those days there were so many sermons both in church and on the radio about the second coming of Christ. The rapture of the church! It was so real to me and seemed so imminent. I feared I would never have the chance to grow up to serve the Lord as a missionary. He would surely come before I could grow up. So I prayed, "Lord, I'm only a child but I really do love you and I want to serve you. What can I do for you NOW?" I was only 12 years old. I got an idea. Up in the granary attic were bushel baskets of old liquor bottles from the former owner. I secretly hauled a bucket of soapy water up there and scrubbed out some of those bottles. (They'd probably be valuable today). I got tracts from the church tract rack and corks from Dad's fishing tackle box. I then tucked those sealed bottles under my jacket and snuck over the hill down to the river and one by one threw those "tract" bottles into the river. I prayed over each bottle that some fisherman would find it, read the tract and trust in Jesus. Night after night I wept and prayed for those bottles. I followed them in my prayers and imagination as they floated down Trade River to the St. Croix River, to the Mississippi and all the way down to New Orleans. Possibilities of changed lives all that way! I don't know if some day in heaven I'll meet someone who found Christ through a tract in a bottle; but it wouldn't surprise me because God does specially answer the prayers of children. These are all just a few sample bits of my unorthodox missionary beginnings.

MISSIONARY MEETINGS

I heard that missionaries were supposed to have a "missionary call". I thought it would be a voice in the night like Samuel heard. I never heard any voice so I never told anyone about my burden for China. Our church would have missionary meetings and they'd give an altar call for young people to dedicate their life for missions. They actually came down the aisle and asked me if I would follow my parent's example and be a missionary. I clammed up, thinking, "Look, brother, this thing isn't inherited! Why don't you pick on someone else? "

I turned seventeen a month before my high school graduation. I knew I'd have to get some training if I were to become a missionary. Even if I never got that missionary "call", Bible school would be useful just to serve God in this country. Due to the example of a Godly gal from our church who I admired, I chose to attend the same school where she'd gone, the Evangelical Free Church Bible Institute in Chicago. A lady in our church had rich relatives living on Chicago's North Shore in a 17-room house on a cliff overlooking Lake Michigan. They wanted cheap labor from the country to help care for their two boys and big house. Their relative in our church approached me with their offer. I jumped at the chance because I didn't want my parents to pay for my schooling. If God were to meet my needs in the future on the mission field, He could start right now! And He did.

LEAVING HOME

My family was shocked at my eagerness to leave the home and farm that I loved. I never told them why. With my small cardboard suitcase and $11.00 that I had earned picking strawberries for five cents a quart, I took the train alone to Chicago and my new job. My family replaced me with a milking machine. God sprinkled my path with surprises, lessons and great experiences, some nothing short of miraculous, by giving me jobs and supplying all my needs in unexpected ways. Through the school I got afternoon and weekend jobs washing clothes, ironing white shirts, cleaning homes, etc. When working in the home of the organist of Moody Church, I was amused to hear myself referred to as "the cleaning lady". I saw myself rather as "a servant of the Most High God!"

For some jobs, like the job of proofreading for Good News Press, I took the elevated train to work in downtown Chicago. God always met my needs, although sometimes just in time. One evening I attended the midweek service at the nearby Lakeview Evangelical Free Church where a "faith missionary" gave her testimony. She had no fixed support. The following day, while studying in the dorm, I felt moved to send her five dollars through that church. I checked my tithe box. It was empty. I looked at my own cash box. It held just one five dollar bill. I needed cash to take the elevated train downtown to work that afternoon; so I went back to my books but I could not concentrate. The thought came, "Send her your five dollars". I argued with God that it would not be very responsible to do that. Since the nagging thought persisted, I took it as God's prompting. So enclosing the bill with a note to the church on how to direct its use, I used my last 3-cent stamp to mail it in the U.S. mail box down the street. I then returned to good focused study.

At noon I walked the few blocks from our dorm to our main building on 4211 Hermitage Avenue where lunch was served. I still worried about how I would get to work that afternoon. I needed two dimes for the round trip "L" train fare to my work downtown. It never occurred to me to borrow when I had no means to repay. I had a set of new short pencils handy for keeping score at board games. I tried to sell them cheap to fellow students. I couldn't tell them why I wanted to sell them. They showed no interest.

After lunch before leaving somehow for work downtown (obviously I couldn't walk it), I checked my mail box. There was a letter from a friend with a $25.00 check enclosed! God had multiplied my gift five times. It was the first but certainly not the last such experience of the Lord providing for me so unexpectedly. God was testing my obedience and proving His faithfulness. <u>But</u> I still hadn't heard any missionary "call".

KENTUCKY EXPERIENCE

Instead of working to pay my bills that first summer's school vacation in 1948, I went down to work with our missionaries in Hazard, Kentucky with the youth camps and vacation Bible classes for kids. I did this for the value of practical experience. In those days no one asked for support for short term missions. You just trusted God for your needs and I wasn't about to ask for support ever. Amazingly I've never had to do that.

A co-worker, Dorothy Kirk, and I taught Sunday schools in churches and several daily vacation Bible schools in school houses. In one church we had to clean up the bat droppings everywhere each Sunday morning before Sunday school began. A retarded young fellow often shadowed us as we walked the paths to our school. That was a bit unnerving.

For one week of DVBS we had to sleep overnight at the school house that had a metal roof. After the daytime classes for children and evening meetings for adults, Dorothy and I locked the doors and turned ourselves in for the night. We would sleep on the school benches. Once unknown to us, some young men, perhaps even a bit tipsy, were waiting in the woods for us to drift off to sleep. Suddenly we were startled awake by a shower of rocks hitting the school's metal roof with a deafening clatter. Quite terrifying! We knew that these mountain folk were known to get drunk and gun happy! Anything could happen but nothing did. PTL! We continued with the DVBS classes and meetings the next day as though nothing had happened. No one could scare us off so easily. The Kentucky experience was valuable although sometimes it was scary like the Wild West.

The missionary gals who worked permanently down there around Hazard, Kentucky were a wonderful example to us. Every morning after breakfast we knelt at our kitchen chairs praying together for the needs and contacts around us. That summer we did see some lives changed by the Gospel. One such young girl Teda, who trusted Christ that summer, eventually joined the Kentucky mission and now 65 years later, though retired and ill, is still laboring for Christ down there.

One wise old Kentucky missionary down there, Richard Carlson, knowing of my burden for China, taught me a truth that influenced my whole ministry. He said, "Doris, there will be plenty of Westerners on the mission field including other missionaries that you can find to fill your social life and be your friends; but the Nationals will be watching you to see with whom you choose to spend your leisure time. By that they will determine whether they are your work or your friends." I never forgot that and it definitely affected my whole ministry and personal relationship choices.

MISSIONARY CALL

One day in Bible School we had a special chapel speaker, Anna Lindgren. She was on the Moody Bible Institute faculty and the author of the Moody Colportage book, "In His Presence." She spoke on knowing God's will and how He guides us step by step. As with a flashlight, you don't need to see your final destination but just your immediate path! It was a great comfort to me and just what I needed. I had been so worried that I would MISS God's will for me. Because she had taught my mother at Moody, she recognized my surname on the list of students. She asked to see me after chapel.

In my conversation with her I shared my burden for China and how I was waiting for that missionary "call." She smiled and said, "God must have called you when you were very young." It was like scales falling from my eyes. Why, of course. The call of God was that burden on my heart from which I could never get away. Not a voice in the night! I promptly thanked the Lord and wrote to our Free Church mission secretary, applying to become a missionary candidate. I got a polite letter in response that said they didn't consider candidates under 21 and I could contact him again in a few years if I was still interested. I had just turned eighteen; so I wrote back, "In case I would still be interested in a few years, where would you have wanted me to have gone to school in the meantime and what would you have wanted me to have studied?" He replied, "A Bible major at Wheaton College".

WHICH COLLEGE?

Wheaton's enrollment was filled with returning WWII veterans. I was seventh on the waiting list when classes began and I didn't have any money. I reasoned, "If God wants me there, He'll supply." He didn't; so I dropped out of school for a semester to work a live-in job for that same family on the North Shore. By this time they were willing to pay me almost anything to have my help. With my room and board supplied as a live-in, I could save all my pay for school costs. Instead of Wheaton College, I chose North Park College for my first two years (Associate of Arts, 2-year degree). It was not as expensive as Wheaton or as competitive to enter.

FUNDING NORTH PARK STUDIES

To fund my North Park studies and pay my bills, I worked in the college kitchen and dining hall plus I did nurses' aid work at Swedish Covenant Hospital. I'll never forget my first day as a nurses' aid when I was called to help prepare a corpse for the morgue. I really enjoyed the opportunity to serve those sick patients as my service to Jesus. I never had to borrow money nor go into debt. During the summer months, I also stayed with a Jewish family, near to North Park where I did housework for them (and learned how to perfectly season steak with garlic). Their seven year old son loved to hear stories about our farm. Once he asked me, "Do your cows give Borden's milk?"

GOOD MISSIONARY TRAINING

When I finally entered Wheaton College as a junior, I applied for kitchen food service work to support myself. When the director asked me which food service job I wanted, I said, "You can give me the job no one else wants to do." She did. I thought that would be good missionary training. How I regretted those words!

That semester I washed about 1,200 drinking glasses following every noon dining hall meal. The glasses often were caked with dried milk or chocolate milk or stuffed with paper napkins or other trash. They had to be hand washed with brushes inside and out, dipped in three batches of hot water with various rinses and stacked to dry. The rinse tubs were low and I was tall. Water was sloshing across the floor from the dish washer machines so I had to stand even higher on boards to keep my feet dry. With my back aching, my hands in hot water for two hours and then heading out in the cold for a 2:00 p.m. class, I could hardly stay awake. I had my well-deserved pity parties (I thought); but that job eventually became a joy as I learned to turn it into a daily worship experience! It became a valuable lesson in how to turn a bad attitude around. It WAS good missionary training after all!

JAPAN INSTEAD?

While I was at Wheaton, the mission contacted me to ask whether I would be willing to go to Japan instead because China was under Communist rule and likely Hong Kong would fall too. The mission had a young single gal headed for Japan and they didn't want to send her alone. Well, I had heard from my folks about all the atrocities the Japanese had inflicted on the Chinese and I identified with the Chinese. My first reaction to the suggestion of going to Japan as a missionary was, "Those Japs, they DESERVE to go to hell." The Lord reminded me, "So do you! I died for the Japanese, too!" God convicted me of my attitude and I responded, "Lord, if you'll put a love for the Japanese in my heart, I'm available even for Japan." For a whole year, I prepared to go to Japan; then a senior missionary from Hong Kong, Arthur Lindquist, came home saying, "Hong Kong is NOT going to fall to the Japanese. We need you in Hong Kong. I realized that this had been a test to show me my heart. My first burden had always been for the Chinese and still was.

Actually long before I was twenty one, I was an accepted candidate for Hong Kong under the Evangelical Free Church mission board. I wanted to go straight to the field after graduation from Wheaton College; but I had no support and the mission required all candidates to attend a week's missionary workshop before going to any field. You had to have full support pledged before you could even attend that workshop in early July. What chance did I have? I wouldn't even graduate until June 16th!

FROM APOLOGY TO SUPPORT

Now in my last semester at Wheaton, God was convicting me of something back in my Bible School days at Free Church Bible Institute. Often when I had my devotions, God's Spirit would remind me of it. The issue went back to my childhood. My stepmother was out of her depth in raising children. We just grew like Topsy, without much training. At Bible School it was obvious that I had many rough edges that needed polishing. We had a dean of women, Mom Carlson, who set about to do that very thing! She was ancient. Over seventy! And a classic Old Maid! She had all the quirks and queers proverbially ascribed to old maids; but she had one redeeming quality. She loved us students and we loved her. She knew my folks, knew I was probably headed for the mission field and she saw in me an "uncut diamond". She proceeded to work on me. You can imagine how I appreciated that! I thought she picked on me. I had my little way of getting back at her. I could imitate her quaint ways so it would bring down the house! It was all done in fun, of course, when she wasn't there. Now when I was getting ready to leave for Hong Kong, God kept bringing that to mind. "You weren't very nice to Mom Carlson, were you?" "Oh, Lord. It was all in fun." The reminders didn't go away. Finally I asked, "Lord, what do you want me to do about it? Go and apologize?" I knew right away that the answer was "yes."

But how embarrassing! How could I tell her? I was committed to obedience so I had no choice. On the first day that I had no classes, I took the whole day off from studying to take a train from Wheaton into Chicago, then the"L" train up to the North Side to our Bible Institute and the dorm where she lived as housemother. I went to apologize. And she wasn't home! I was delighted. Well, I'd done what I could.

At my next Quiet Time, the Lord bugged me again. "But I did try!" "You could WRITE her an apology!" So, difficult as it was, I did it and mailed it. I got the sweetest letter back. She didn't know and it didn't matter. I was forgiven. Little did I know that she was on the mission board of the large Summerdale Free Church that I had been attending while in Bible School! My apology reminded her that I was headed for Hong Kong.

I had just finished my last final exam when someone handed me a note to call this number. It was the Summerdale Free Church to tell me that their missions committee had met and decided to cover my full missionary support! Now I could attend that July workshop and head out for Hong Kong with no delays for raising support! I got a powerful lesson that I had better obey God immediately whenever He speaks!

FINAL STRUGGLE

The Sunday night before leaving home, I went through a struggle. My parents and my brother were sound asleep but I could not sleep. It was a few days before my scheduled return to the field. I went out into the warm moonlit summer night. The moonlight bathed our farm buildings, the tree covered hillside, the swamp and our white house so brightly in the moonlight. The sounds of our cows munching mouthfuls of grass nearby and a chorus of croaking frogs in the swamp were the only sound that beautiful night. It occurred to me that by my first furlough it would never be like this again. Things would change. My brother was of marriage age and my parents were old. Our home would never be the same again. I struggled between my love for God and love for my home and family. Then I looked at the moon and thought that the same moon shines in Hong Kong. More important the God behind this moon will be with me in Hong Kong and with my family here. I surrendered to God and peace filled my heart. I left for the field with eager joy.

FREIGHTER TO HONG KONG

On September 23, 1953, I boarded a freighter for Hong Kong. I traveled with a fellow missionary, Ruth Sundquist, who was returning for her second term. I had said my goodbyes to family and traveled by train, a 3-day trip to the West coast. Dad had coached me, "Food on the train is very expensive. You watch around meal time when the train stops and the staff gets off at unscheduled stops and then you get off. You follow them to where they go to eat and get back on board when they do." It worked!

Our freighter carried only four passengers--Ruth and me plus a missionary couple with another mission. The trip would take a full month because the ship had to stop at ports to load and unload cargo. This gave us time for fellowship and prayer together.

SHOCKING NEWS

We four passengers had several days' wait before leaving San Francisco. While we waited, Ruth received a shocking letter from our Evangelical Free Church mission's director. It enclosed a letter from Ruth's furlough doctor stating that her liver was still full of amoeba. (This had been a problem on her first term. A problem she hoped had now been solved.) The doctor's letter was postmarked two months previous to this, and no one knew how or where it had gotten stuck for two months in the postal system. If the mission board had known sooner, they would not have let her return to Hong Kong yet. Since we were already aboard ship, she could decide herself whether to stay for more treatments or sail now. Her immediate response was, "I'm going!" She was available and eager to return.

Here's a bit of background on Ruth. She had already completed one four year term which was mostly given to language study. Her term had started in Canton until the Communists took China and our missionaries had fled to British controlled Hong Kong. During that term she got very run down and sick. Her Hong Kong doctor found that she had tuberculosis (TB) of the glands which was caused by amoeba in her liver which sapped her vitality. Surgery could remove the TB glands; but unless she got rid of the amoeba in her liver, the tuberculosis would return. So her number one goal that first furlough had been to rid her liver of the amoeba. Her furlough doctor gave her repeated doses of de-worming medicine, each stronger than the last, until she was on the verge of ulcers. Now her situation seemed hopeless. With the amoebae still sapping her energy, her tuberculosis of the glands was bound to recur. Any further anti-amoeba treatment would surely give her ulcers.

HEALING PRAYER

We four missionaries discussed this problem together as we traveled. We decided to each pray for guidance whether or not we should ask God for her healing from the liver amoeba. After some days of individually praying for guidance, we compared notes. We all felt assured that she would be healed of the amoeba if we so prayed. We anointed her forehead with mosquito oil according to James 5, knelt and thanked God for healing her. From then on we felt such confidence that we just assumed she had been healed.

Upon our arrival in Hong Kong, Ruth returned to her same doctor who had first discovered her amoeba. She took test after test. No amoeba was ever found again! Ruth continued her missionary career until retirement age with no sign of TB, amoeba or ulcers. I saw God answer prayer for healing before I ever set foot in Hong Kong. My Orient adventures were just beginning.

ARRIVAL IN HONG KONG

Our freighter arrived in the Hong Kong harbor October 23rd one month from our departure from San Francisco. Fellow missionaries first gave me a one week tour and introduction to the colony before I landed on one of Hong Kong's 350 islands where I was to begin my 9-month Robinson Crusoe days. There on Cheung Chau Island, I would live alone immersed in a strange language amid a strange culture with no one with whom to speak English. My motivation to learn language was KEEN.

There were no Chinese language schools back then. I was told that Chinese has no alphabet and Cantonese has nine different tones. At twenty three years of age I was in for the biggest adventure of my life!

Psalm 57:7, 9, 10.
7. My heart is steadfast, O God, my heart is steadfast.
9. I will praise you, O Lord, among the nations; I will sing of you among the peoples. May your glory be over all the earth!
10. For great is your love, reaching to the heavens; your faithfulness reaches to the skies. Be exalted, O God, above the heavens; let your glory be over all the earth.

Chapter 3

ADVENTURES BEYOND EXPECTATION

The Covenant Retirement Village Vesper talks forced me to rethink and put down on paper some of God's blessings, lessons, human interest memories that came to mind, (not necessarily chronologically) as well as some of God's dealings in my own life. Without the time constraints of a talk, I have here added to the Vespers examples more of God's fantastic answers to prayer, His sense of humor, His perfect timing and His working through <u>available</u> lives. I pray that my sharing in this way will be more than entertainment, will strengthen your trust in God and increase your desire to serve Him. He is surely worthy of our trust.

I feel incredibly blessed to have had the privilege of four decades of seeing Him work through many lives in Hong Kong and elsewhere. I want Him to be glorified in all that I share with you here.

Psalm 26: 2-3

2. Test me, O LORD, and try me, examine my heart and my mind;

3. For your love is ever before me, and I walk continually in your truth.

Psalm 86:10-11
10. For you are great and do marvelous deeds; you alone are God.
11. Teach me your way, O LORD, and I will walk in your truth; give me an undivided heart, that I may fear your name.

ARRIVAL IMPRESSIONS

Our ship pulled into Hong Kong's busy fascinating harbor, October 23, 1953. That was one month to the day since Ruth Sundquist and I had left the States by freighter. The Hong Kong harbor was full of ships that like ours docked at a buoy out in the harbor. Missionaries and Chinese friends of Ruth filled several walla walla motorized water taxis that surrounded our ship. These water taxis, which we would use to reach land, rose and sank with the waves. The reason that I even mention this ride from our ship to shore is because on that walla walla, Mrs. Don Carlson, one of our senior missionaries, challenged me with an opportunity that I couldn't refuse. She asked me if I'd be willing to teach an English Sunday School class for young people. This English Sunday School was expected to start soon in our book store. Of course, I was delighted and eager to promise, anticipating a ministry opportunity even before I had learned Chinese. This was a promise that would return to haunt me a year later as I'll explain.

I made a mental note that first week (nearly November) that never in my life had I perspired so much! I was puzzled. October was supposed to be the start of the cool fall season! I was continually wet due to a level of humidity, PLUS heat that I had never experienced in the Mid-West, not even in Chicago.

ORIENTATION

That first week in Hong Kong was orientation to my new world. I stayed with the single missionary gals and slept on the fourth floor balcony of their five-story building (no elevator). My bed was a camp cot made up each night and dismantled each morning to give us room. This continued to be my weekend rest stop for the next nine months.

During that first week, life was a whirl of bewildering activities in very unfamiliar surroundings. Strange sights, sounds and smells brought back long forgotten memories of my childhood in China, like bits of a dream coming back after a sound sleep.

Here hawkers called out their wares or services loud enough so people on the upper floors would hear and come down for business. "Knives and scissors sharpened here", "will fix shoes," etc. My favorite was a cry every night after dark that sounded like, "Oh me! Oh my!" It really announced, "Have padded quilts for sale".

HONG KONG DESCRIBED

The gals explained that the name, Kowloon, means nine dragons from the appearance of the range of low mountains behind the city. The Kowloon peninsula that juts out into the harbor about three square miles and is densely populated was the focus of most of our mission work at that time.

Kowloon was just one of the three main parts of the British colony of Hong Kong. Behind the mountains and the city of Kowloon were the New Territories that stretched 24 miles to the Chinese border. It was mainly rural lowland with small farm plots on which grew flowers, vegetables, geese and ducks.

Victoria Island, called by the locals "the Hong Kong side", was across the harbor and our "downtown" with its large commercial buildings and multiple rows of tram tracks for easy double-decker transportation. This main island is about fifteen miles long, two to five miles wide and 1,500 ft. high. It is a mountain circled by roads that wind around like cow paths to the top.

About 350 smaller rocky islands, mostly uninhabitable, but contributing to a very ideal harbor, make up the rest of the colony. A few of these islands had enough soil or flat land to support a fishing village. These islands were connected to the main island and Kowloon peninsula by a network of cheap ferries. One of these, Cheung Chau Island, was shaped like a dumbbell for which it was nicknamed. It was to become my first home in Hong Kong.

This colony of Hong Kong was leased in 1898 for 99 years from China by the British as war booty for winning the Opium War. For financial gain, Britain had sought to force opium on China. China's fishing junks were no match for the British navy; so when the lease expired in 1997, the British returned Hong Kong to China. They really had no option because the colony had grown way beyond "Boundary Street" and the water supply was on the Chinese side.

MY HOUSING

There was much discussion among the missionaries about where I should live. There were no flats available to rent. Refugees were pouring into Hong Kong from China and even the sidewalks were crowded with families sleeping on pieces of cardboard. Refugee family units were divided by partial walls made out of cardboard boxes. Upper stories of buildings, built out over the sidewalks and flush with the street, gave rain protection to the sidewalks and refugees.

A senior missionary, Arthur Lindquist, offered me his house out on Cheung Chau Island. This dumbbell shaped island had steep terraced hills where the local farmers grew vegetables. Every morning and evening they watered and fertilized these terraces with "honey bucket water" as their aroma wafted across the valley. This island, soon to become my home, was about an hour and a half ferry ride from the city on the Kowloon peninsula.

The Japanese had torn down the concrete-stone summer houses on the island's hills. These houses were formerly owned by well-to-do foreigners. The Japanese wanted the iron reinforcement rods in the concrete for their military. Mr. Lindquist had the foresight to buy cheaply one of these torn down units and had the stone house rebuilt and offered it to me. Our other missionaries protested, "You can't put a new young missionary girl who doesn't even know the language alone out on an island!" I was twenty three. There were thirty thousand Chinese living below the steep hills in the fishing village at the waterfront edge; but I couldn't converse with them. I realized living there would be a marvelous language learning opportunity. With no viable alternative, my pleas for this "ideal setup" carried the day. Because that was my own request, I could hardly complain how lonely I sometimes felt between weekends when I returned to the city with our other missionaries.

SUNDAY SHOCKS

On my first Sunday there, I visited a Chinese Church. I sat in the back row which was just one step indoors from the sidewalk open market. I understood not a word of the sermon but noticed to my amusement that all heads in the place were the same color--black! Suddenly a breathless man, in farm-shorts, thongs and straw hat, rushed in and plopped down beside me with his bushel basket full of squirming live shrimp! Surprises everywhere! I was to learn later that he had slipped in, not out of spiritual hunger, but because the police were raiding the market just outside the church and searching for unlicensed hawkers like him.

LOST IN THE DARK

On that first Sunday after my week's introduction to Kowloon City, missionary friends accompanied me by ferry-boat and path to introduce me to my new island stone house. Dumbbell Island possessed no roads, just a zigzag path between village buildings on the water front and up a steep hill to house #23 that was about to become my new home! That afternoon I had to learn the layout of Dumbbell Island at least enough to find my way back all alone after dark later that night.

The Chinese mission was giving a delicious welcome feast for Ruth and me, the new arrivals, on that Sunday evening. Because my language classes were scheduled to start at my island house the next morning, I had to return by myself later that night after the feast.

"You're sure you can find your way back here by yourself tonight?" "Absolutely"! I hadn't counted on how different things would look in the dark. There were no streetlights or roads, only paths. I had only my flashlight as I climbed the steep hill above the village below. Not noticing in the dark the fork in the path, I took the wrong way. Soon it was obvious to me that this was NOT the path that I'd walked that afternoon. I wandered helplessly above and around a soccer field that was carved flat between hills. It was about 11:00

p.m., pitch dark, and I was lost on this island not knowing a word of Chinese! What could I do?

I prayed, of course; then I noticed a man on the pathway ahead of me. Taking this stranger to be the answer to my prayer, I ran to catch up with him and tried to talk to him in English. He just motioned me to follow him. I had no other option. Eventually we came to steep steps leading up to a concrete foreign house. He knocked on the door and, when it opened, I fell into the arms of Mrs. Stuart Gunzel! The Gunzels were our fellow missionaries who ministered to the Mongols on the Mongolian pasture lands and to whom we brought supplies when I was a child, nearly twenty years before!

The Gunzels had been living and working on my island of Cheung Chau with four Mongol scholars to revise the Mongolian New Testament. They had left Mongolia due to the Communist take-over. With the revision of the New Testament finally completed, they were packing to leave Hong Kong. I spent that night with them, awed and overwhelmed by God's loving provision and perfect timing—His amazing delightful answer to His lost child's prayer.

ROBINSON CRUSOE DAYS

I soon learned of some unique features of my new home. It was built with cement blocks and rocks plastered with cement inside and out. The inside walls were whitewashed with the floor made of plain concrete. No amount of effort on my part could mop the floor dry, for like me, it, was simply sweating—in this case with condensation. Fortunately, this house overlooked the ocean with its multiple fishing vessels and was blessed with sea breezes and a fantastic view.

My new home had florescent light tubes which hung from the high ceiling by wires and in the kitchen two individual kerosene burners for the cook stove. The water supply came from rain-water caught on the flat roof and stored in a tank above the ceiling. From there rain water was piped down to a concrete sink in the kitchen. A pipe from the ceiling brought water to a tiny corner porcelain sink in the bathroom which drained into a bucket below to be reused to flush the toilet. Toilet water was recycled again by flowing into a tank in the garden below for watering and fertilizing the luxuriant vegetables and flowers. I felt like I was in the Garden of Eden!

HOUSE AND LANGUAGE HELP

The missionaries had arranged for a village lady, Ah-Fan, to come every day to go to the market, buy food and cook for me so I could focus on language study and not be completely alone by day. Unfortunately, she spoke a different village dialect than I was learning.

The mission also hired a village man, who had some language teaching experience, to come for three hours, five days a week to teach me Cantonese. He spoke only broken English.

Ah Fan would ask me what I wanted to eat. My language teacher wrote for me in phonetics (we called it Romanized Cantonese) the names of several possible dishes. He was never there at my mealtimes; so I would forget to ask him again to suggest some other dish for variety. As a result, I ate the same topping on my rice three times a day every day. It seemed forever. One day when Ah Fan asked me again what to fix for the next meal, I could feel resentment rising inside me over the continuing sameness. I blurted out in English "Raisin pie!" She repeated "Pie, Pie!" (Apparently I had said it using the same tones when she had first learned "pie".) Because she had cooked for foreigners before, she knew the word "Pie"; but "raisin" drew a blank. I got a brainstorm! I noticed a resemblance to raisins in all the dead flies that I had swatted that were still lying scattered on the table so I pointed to a dead fly and repeated, "Raisin pie!" She looked aghast, then chuckled, and trundled off down to the market. Believe it or not, she came up that day with a real raisin pie for me!

LANGUAGE STUDY

I recognized that as a missionary, my top priorities must be my communication with God and verbal communication with the people that I had come to reach. The language teacher that the mission had arranged for me came five mornings a week to my house for three hours of class. First he drilled me on the nine tones in Cantonese until eventually I could distinguish the difference between them. I tape-recorded everything he said and imitated the recording over and over until I had it sounding perfect to me, no matter how long that took. My teacher had pages of practical conversation dialogues written phonetically for tonal practice, which I recorded, practiced and memorized cold from my tape recordings. I would practice these memorized sentences on the Chinese down in the village with some comical results.

For example, identical sounds expressed on a different tone or pitch could mean either a priest, very bitter or difficult, a new pair of trousers, or a bride. Following my tape recording, I would pronounce each phrase with correct tone until I thought I had it perfect. I'd then practice that phrase 20 times, counting on my fingers, doing it faster and faster for fluency. I'd do the same with the next phrase 20 times, then the two phrases together another 20 times, etc. I soon memorized them. These conversation dialogues became very useful in practical situations.

Having no one else to converse with, I was highly motivated to study and practice Cantonese. After my teacher left for the day, I'd study until at last, my book would drop from my fingers to the floor from sheer exhaustion.

Sometimes I'd climb down to the shore below my house and sit on the huge boulders to study my character cards with the roar of the ocean waves splashing around me. I was awed by God's creative genius and glory. I'd wonder what God had in store for me forty years down the road as I served Him there.

LANGUAGE BOO-BOOS

Often in the afternoon I'd go down to the village to try out my Cantonese. I remember going to a likely shop to try to buy some fertilizer for my house plants. I wrote down the Romanized term that my teacher gave me but I forgot to mark the tones. I should have said Fei Liu. I asked using the right sound but with a tone which meant "bird's". The store personnel were politely solemn in my presence as I tried all the possible tone combinations before them but I failed to hit the right ones. When they thought I was out of earshot, I heard them burst into peals of uncontrollable laughter.

I concluded that my language errors would be more readily forgiven if I made them early on; so I tried to boldly use my Chinese whenever possible. The result was ever so many laughs. For example, my teacher taught me how to ask, "What is his name?" When at some company's house I tried to ask for their dog's name, they burst out laughing for I had used the most polite idiomatic way of asking "What is his honorable surname" as though he was a family member. In China their dogs are just DOGS and not loved as we cherish pets. It was an insult.

When our Chinese Christian workers came to my island once for a day of fellowship together at a waterfront outdoor tarp-covered eating place over the water, I saw my language teacher in the same "restaurant". I tried to introduce him to our co-workers, saying, "This is my teacher". Although my terms were correct, I used them in an idiomatic form that really said, "This is my husband". He turned all shades of red while my Chinese friends tried to hide their laughter behind handkerchiefs. Years later there was another example when I was trying to learn Mandarin and the teacher asked me to say in Mandarin, "I want to light the stove". With only one slight vowel error in one word, what I said meant "I'm about to give birth to a donkey."

FIRST SERMON

Obviously if you are to learn Cantonese, language study must be your first priority **most of your first four-year term**. That just lays a foundation. English ministry can get in the way of that task. There was no language school at that time and I had no schedule to follow. After those first nine months on the island, it was easy for me to get involved in ministry while fitting in time with a language teacher a couple times a week. For that I had to take a walla walla (a small putt- boat) across the harbor to my teacher's flat. Although ministry is more enjoyable than language study, I found a way to combine both.

I remember my first big language adventure. Just nine months after arriving in Hong Kong, I was asked to speak to our entire combined youth fellowship group from all our seven churches, probably a couple hundred youth. No doubt they expected me to speak through an interpreter. Although I was painfully aware of how pitifully limited my Cantonese vocabulary was, I was determined to give my talk in Cantonese. I remember my subject, *"That I may know Christ in the fellowship of His sufferings"* from Phil. 3:10.

First I prepared my message and then I typed it word for word in English. Next, because I wanted to say it exactly the way a Chinese would phrase it rather than in English word order, I got a Chinese friend, who was an excellent interpreter, to interpret after me sentence by sentence as though we were in a real church service while I tape-recorded it all. Back home as I listened to the tape, I typed out the whole message, this time in Romanized Cantonese. Next I marked all the tones, underlined all the new vocabulary (and there was plenty of that) and then went over it with my language teacher. He checked for tone mark errors and gave me meanings for all the new vocabulary which I then had to learn. I memorized the whole thing and gave it in Cantonese to the amazement of my colleagues and audience who knew how very new I was at Cantonese. What they didn't know was how many hours and days went into the preparation. I found this a very useful method to learning the language besides sparing our Chinese friends the pain of hearing us Westerners speak their language in our own way. I continued using this method for all message preparation throughout my whole first four-year term and also much of my second term. I was intensely motivated to learn and had stumbled upon excellent learning strategies, thanks to the faithful prayers of my many prayer partners.

That hard work paid off as the following humorous incident reveals. Many years later, FEBC (Far East Broadcasting Co.) asked me to help them mail a Bible to a listener in interior China who had requested one. Mailing it from Hong Kong would not do. It must be mailed from within China if it were to reach its destination. After an hour's train ride to the border and going through immigration, customs, etc., I crossed into China and found a post office to mail my Bible. It was wrapped and addressed; but it must first be opened, checked and rewrapped by the postal clerk before mailing it. This was no problem because the clerk had no idea what a Bible was. While she rewrapped it, the clerk out of curiosity struck up a conversation with me. She asked me, "Are you mailing it back to the home village?" The question seemed so odd. I just nodded. Then she asked "You're from Hong Kong, aren't you? And you've lived there a long time, haven't you?" After this exchange, she concluded "Do you realize that you have lived out there among those Westerners so long, you have grown to **LOOK** like a Westerner!" Although I sure didn't look like one, she had actually taken me for a Chinese! When I grasped her meaning, I gulped in surprise and I thanked God for His help with that difficult language.

I should here add a caveat regarding my grasp of Chinese characters. Since I observed that children learn to speak long before they can read or write I felt that I should focus on spoken Cantonese rather than get side-tracked by characters! No language school or missionaries were supervising my study so it was many years later before I taught myself characters. As a result I was never very proficient in reading Chinese other than in the Bible.

FIRST CHRISTMAS PROGRAM

Two months after my arrival I celebrated my first Christmas in Hong Kong. The streets were crowded with refugees from China, sleeping on the sidewalks in make-shift shelters of cardboard. I saw few signs of Christmas. It was not commercialized; but it took very little to draw a crowd. Refugee children swarmed everywhere carrying younger brothers and sisters on their backs.

Our Grace Free Church Sunday School Christmas program was celebrated in the church ground floor sanctuary beside a busy intersection. The back wall of the sanctuary was simply folding doors that opened to the street. When this whole back wall opened, children poured in and filled the sanctuary—a crowd of noisy kids extending way out into the street and pushing to get in. With babies on their backs, they stood to see, even climbing up on the benches and pushing up the aisles. It was more like a circus than a Sunday School program.

We had no microphones in those days so the chatter and commotion drowned out the whole program. I was assigned the task of keeping order! Oh, I got their attention all right but not as I had hoped. I knew no Chinese this early. I did what any American would do. I said a loud, "Shhhhhh! Shhhhhh! "That brought down the house because this was the typical mother's command when holding a baby without a diaper over the curb to induce a wet response! Such a command at such a time, instead of silence, brought peals of uncontrollable laughter that drowned out everything!

Years later when I was helping in our Living Springs Church which met on the first floor above the street, another unexpected guest nearly broke up the Christmas program while the children were performing on the platform.

The church kitchen had typical open gutters and drains so live-in cockroaches were inevitable. Our young people solved that problem by putting two turtles in the kitchen to control the bug population. The turtles required no care. They fed themselves. We seldom saw them as they were usually under the sink and cement shelves doing their job. Once when the youth were painting the small church sanctuary in beige, one mischievous teen wiped his brush on one turtle's back. A beige turtle!

When should this freak turtle choose to show himself but during one Christmas program! The church was packed with guests and the children were on the platform saying their pieces. Out came this beige turtle from the kitchen, lumbering down the center aisle toward the platform to the astonishment of the guests and giggles of the performing children! Apparently he wanted to get in on the action! Was this God's sense of humor again?

FRIDAY NIGHT ENGLISH BIBLE CLASS

Every Friday afternoon I'd take the ferries necessary to reach Kowloon, the part of Hong Kong where our missionaries lived. What a relief to talk in English again! After my first Christmas there, one of our missionary gals, Helen Johnson, had to leave for furlough; so she asked me to take her regular Friday evening English Bible Class. I was careful to tell her that I'd pray about it first. I did so and felt a real peace about taking it. I had a great time in that class of about six or eight high school or post high school students. Coming from English schools, they had excellent English. They had a heart for God and we became close friends. Five sisters lived in a flat across the street from Grace Church. Several were in my English Bible class. Their home became my second home. Outside of that class, they never spoke English to me. This forced me to use my Cantonese and they corrected me where I needed it. A great help!

Esther was the middle sister and in her first year of teaching. She was the one that I was mentoring and I was closest to her. She was the chairman of their church youth group of about 60 consisting of mostly high school youth. I would join their Saturday night youth meetings and although I had little vocabulary to interact with most of them, I felt strongly drawn to them, especially to the English speakers.

Some fellow missionaries told me that those were good kids whose social life centered in the church; but there was little evidence in the lives of many of them that they had a personal relationship with Jesus Christ. This troubled me and often the Holy Spirit so moved in my heart to pray for them that I had to set aside my language books, which I was so motivated to study, and drop to my knees to cry out to God in prayer for these youth. The burden was so heavy that I sensed God was sharing with me His heart for them. I prayed for a heaven sent spiritual revival that would turn their lives around to a great love for Jesus and a commitment to total obedience to Him. I sent letters home asking others to pray, too.

GETHSEMANE

It was my custom on Saturday mornings, after my Friday night Bible class in town, to go early by bus out beyond the city to the mountain foothills. There was a place that was easy to climb up to, with scrub pines and big rocks. Many had Scripture verses scratched or painted on them. It was a place that was frequented by Christians for prayer so many nicknamed it "Gethsemane". I went there on Saturday mornings for my own Quiet Time with the Lord and especially for extended prayer time for those members of my Friday night English Bible class.

It occurred to me one day to invite Esther to come along some Saturday morning. She did so regularly after that. After our time with the Lord, we shared our discoveries in the Word and then she corrected her school papers while I studied my Cantonese.

About this time, it looked like the Communists would likely take Hong Kong from the British. There was great fear in the colony. A planned youth retreat was canceled, lest the youth be far away from their parents when Communist China would occupy Hong Kong.

CAPTURED!

One Saturday morning Esther and I climbed to Gethsemane and sat for a while on a bluff that overlooked the highway and the airport below us. It was quite chilly. Because I had no slacks, I had brought along my bright florescent pink PJ bottoms which I donned up there under my wool skirt. There was no one else there to see us. Esther shared some of the scary things that she remembered about the war time when the Japanese had occupied Hong Kong for three years and eight months. We were both studying the book of Revelation and preparing our hearts for times of persecution. We paid little attention when the air raid siren went off, thinking it was just practice preparation for war. We then scattered for our time individually with God. I couldn't see Esther but I knew approximately where she was.

About a half hour later the silence was suddenly broken by sharp commands and I was surrounded by troops in uniform with their guns pointing at me! One of them went to search for any others and came back with Esther with her hands also held up signifying surrender.

The Communist invasion had always been my deepest fear. Now I sensed that it had actually happened. They had taken Hong Kong and now had come to round us up! To me this was the end of the world! Yet my heart was flooded with indescribable peace. While the soldiers were communicating in another language, I asked Esther softly under my breath, "How do you feel?" She answered "It seems like such a useless way to die. It's not even a testimony."

The soldiers marched us down the rocky slope to the road below. We had to help each other climb down because it was so steep. We managed to get a few words between us in the process. Esther said, "It can't be the Communists. It's not their uniform!" Although we were still puzzled, that brought great relief from the tension we had just experienced. The soldiers marched us across the highway and toward the airport. With our hands held high with three soldiers ahead of us and three behind, all with their guns in hand, we were quite a sight. Suddenly we both noticed that, as cars stopped to let us cross, my bright pink PJ bottoms were hanging below my skirt and the incongruity of it all hit our funny bone. We were so overcome with inner laughter that we could hardly walk!

We were marched into an airport barracks and the soldiers reported in English to an officer, "We found them up on the hill". I asked, "What have we done? How long will you keep us?" They replied, "It may be two hours or it may be two days". We had no way to contact our families and we had responsibilities on Sunday that we couldn't get to. They examined our small wicker baskets in which we had our Bibles, language books and papers to be corrected. "What's this?" they asked about my Bible. I said, "It's my Bible". They finally decided, yeah, it was a real Bible all right. After two hours they came, apologized and released us. I was still curious over what had happened. They had taken us for spies up on that bluff spying on their air raid practice. They were mercenary Gerka troops working for the British who were doing an air raid practice. The Communists never did take Hong Kong. In my heart they **had** come and at that moment I found God's overwhelming grace and peace. It was a precious lesson to me that should such a crisis come, God's peace will be there. I never needed to fear the Communist take-over again. Eventually, a number of girls from Grace Church would join us there at "Gethsemane" on Saturday forenoons for extended Quiet Times and sharing.

INNER GUILT

About a year into my Hong Kong experience, that English Sunday School that I had heard about on the walla walla from our ship to shore and had promised to help to teach, finally materialized. All those months I had suffered a guilt trip. Why had I so quickly promised Mrs. Carlson that I'd help teach that class before I had prayed about it? How did I know God wanted me to do that task? I was thankful for the long delay; but now it was to start. It would meet in our bookstore. I had promised and I was too new to object. There were two classes. My interest was with the teens but I was given the junior kids. My class was a flop from the beginning. I dreaded Sunday mornings at 9:30. I thought God could not bless that class because I had not asked God's permission about taking it.

After a few months, another Free Church asked me to begin an English Sunday School at their place at 8:00 a.m. I could use the same material as at the bookstore class that followed. Well, I sure prayed about it this time and felt definite peace in taking this added class. I found the 8:00 a.m. class a real blessing. Even using the same material, the 9:30 class was still a complete drag as I struggled with guilt feelings.

At the mission council meeting nearing my first year teaching that class there, I requested to drop that bookstore English Sunday School class and instead sit in on some Chinese classes meeting at that hour to build my Bible vocabulary. My request was perfectly logical and my request passed; but the Carlsons were not happy about it. At that time, I was living in town with them. Mrs. Carlson said to me that evening, "Don and I were disappointed in you today, Doris". I said, "Well, I need to learn Cantonese Bible vocabulary". She replied, "I don't think that was the REAL reason you wanted to quit your class." I burst into tears and confessed my real reason was my feelings of guilt for having promised without prayer first.

We had a wonderful time of prayer together and she helped me learn a most valuable lesson. No matter what wrong step we may have taken, God's full forgiveness and blessing are always available immediately as soon as we come to him with our fault. Having studied God's Word so many years, how could I have missed that truth! For years to come I was to counsel many individuals who had made mistakes far worse than that. I could assure them of God's immediate forgiveness and blessing upon their lives as soon as they repented.

PRAYER BURDEN LIFTED

During my first four year term in Hong Kong, I focused on language learning and building relationships, especially with the youth of Grace Church where I had my Friday night English Bible class and regularly attended their youth fellowship meetings. Although my Cantonese was still very limited, I could pray. By then I had long been burdened for a spiritual revival among them.

One day while praying for them, I was suddenly flooded with a joyful assurance that those prayers were already answered! It was as good as done, although I had no idea when I'd see it. From then on, I could only praise Him in advance.

When revival came, it impacted far beyond my expectations. I had never seen the Holy Spirit move so deeply—especially in a culture that normally withholds outward expressions of emotion. All our prayers were wonderfully answered during a Christmas retreat just one year into my first term.

FIRST WINTER RETREAT

The Grace Church youth group booked a small rural chapel near the China border for three days of meetings. Besides the benches on the ground floor, Zion Chapel had a "U" shaped balcony which served as our men's and women's dormitories. Wires were strung on each side on which a few sheets and blankets were hung up to provide privacy. This was not important because we mostly slept on the balcony benches in the same clothes that we wore during the day.

The youth set aside a large block of time each morning for personal devotions. This was a real luxury for busy students in the quiet country setting. A morning message was followed by small group Bible studies. Afternoons were free for rest, meditation, fun or fellowship before an evening service. The retreat theme was Rev. 12:11 *"They overcame him by the blood of the Lamb and by the word of their testimony and they loved not their lives unto the death."*

REVIVAL AT LAST

Their committee planned a camp fire dedication service after the evening meeting for the last night. After supper one girl suggested that we should meet for a pre-service prayer meeting in the gazebo nearby before the evening service began. While about eight of us girls were praying there, the Holy Spirit began to move that group to earnest prayer. When time came for the evening service to begin, I tried to close our prayer meeting with my first prayer in Chinese! It didn't work. As soon as I finished, the girls continued praying until the evening service was over. The whole group then gathered around the bonfire where they were encouraged to throw a fagot on the fire as they shared with the group a new step of obedience resulting from the retreat.

HOLY SPIRIT CONVICTION

As that service began, I was suddenly smitten with a conviction by the Holy Spirit. When I was teaching in the English Sunday School, I had been unfaithful in handling the offering money. The economy was terrible and the pupils were so poor that their offerings were around ten cents each in local currency. I would dump their offering into my purse with my change and a slip showing their total, around $1.20 each Sunday. Sometimes I'd lose that slip so I'd put in extra to make up for my carelessness. It wasn't the amount that mattered. I had been an unfaithful steward of God's money and I was ashamed to admit that. Nor did I have the Cantonese vocabulary to voice it to the group; but I had to obey the Spirit's prompting. I stood to say that I was under conviction of sin but I hadn't the vocabulary to confess it in Cantonese. I would do so in English before our mission council at my first opportunity which I did. Immediately, Esther, the group's chairman, jumped to her feet in the flickering fire light to confess that she as their chairman had lied to the group. When they were voting on a time change for their regular meetings, their vote was tied. Because she wanted the vote to go one way, she had knowingly counted one hand twice. "So I as your leader have lied to this group. Will you forgive me?"

THE FIRE SPREAD

For the rest of the evening, the kids were confessing what the Spirit had showed them--gossip, grudges, hard feelings, lies, jealousy, etc. until the meeting was closed to facilitate individuals handling issues between themselves. There were tears and hugs and forgiveness. This continued until 2:00 in the morning. Old accounts were being settled and relationships made right as the love of God flowed through the group. The change in the atmosphere was awesome. The young people returned to the city, to their homes and church as a transformed group. There were more things to be made right with the pastor and choir director. The whole church was impacted. The results continued for years. Only God's Spirit could have sparked this revival. It was a wonderful experience for a new missionary who barely was able to understand what was happening. I saw the value of extended prayer and of sharing burdens with faithful prayer partners.

UNFORGETTABLE MACAO TRIP

We were five single missionary gals in our mission and we'd have a ball when we got together, especially when the three Chinese single gals working in our mission joined us. Martha was the parish worker in Grace Church. She was burdened for her idol-worshipping elder sister who lived in Macao, a Portuguese territory that was a night's boat ride from Hong Kong. We all had a standing invitation from Martha's sister, Mrs. So, to visit them in Macao and to take a meal with them. Socially Mrs. So was very friendly; but spiritually she was a hard nut to crack. Martha suggested that the eight of us meet regularly a few Saturday mornings to pray for Mrs. So that her heart would be prepared by the Holy Spirit. So we did. After about six Saturdays of very precious times of prayer together, Martha said, "I feel the time is ripe to accept her invitation.

We set a date, took a night boat with sleeper quarters, and arrived in Macao by morning. First we went to the So residence to say we had arrived. They eagerly invited us back for dinner that evening. We did the tourist thing on Macao that day and visited the famous sites. Macao, a Portuguese colony, was populated by the Chinese and famous for its many casinos. It has long been known as the Las Vegas of the Orient. It boasted about the ruins from an old Catholic church. Only the ornate front remains with its cross on top pointing skyward. It was that cross on that church front that inspired a Christian governor of Hong Kong years ago, while passing by Macao on board ship, to pen the words that became the old hymn, "In the Cross of Christ I Glory" (words by John Bowring; music by Ithamar Conkey). With mixed feelings we visited this tourist site which is now just a shell of the message that the cross represents. It did not take long to circle the island by taxi (I've done it since by bike) to view all the Portuguese styled buildings and tourist sites.

We arrived at the So residence for dinner that evening. The unvarnished floor boards in that home had been scrubbed until they were almost white. There was a large idol shelf with food being offered to the gods. The air was thick with smoke from all the incense being burned to the idols. The eight of us gals joined the So family to sit around a large round table for the special meal. It seemed so ironic to pray asking God to bless the food when all that incense to the idols was burning around us and filling the air with thick smoke.

AN UNUSUAL MEAL

We were in for a special twelve-course meal. This family had once been well-off but no more; yet they went out of their way to really give us a special spread. The first course that they brought out was the most important. It was a large juicy cabbage and meat dish with fresh white Dahlia petals sprinkled on top. I had never before eaten snake; but although it was skinned, the markings of snake scales were visible on the meat! That was an expensive poisonous snake. They believe the poison is in the bones so it was a day's work to prepare it. They had carefully picked off all the meat so no bone would be left in the dish. If only she hadn't told us that the other meat was Cat!

We American single gals hardly dared catch each other's eye as Mrs. So filled our bowls with cat and snake meat! I decided to get it down real quick without having to taste it; but that was a mistake. They came around with seconds! "Was it good? Did you like it?" We had to say it was good. We were their guests. We couldn't say that we were full because this was just the first course of a twelve course meal. I made the second bowl last until that dish was taken off the table and the next course came. Was it delicious? Conflicting emotions ruled out an objective answer.

REASONING WITH THE BLIND

At the end of this otherwise very delicious meal, Martha stood up to officially address her sister, Mrs. So. She told her how Jesus' death on the cross and His shed blood was the payment for our sins. We can have forgiveness of sin and be restored to a love relationship with God as our Father. Mrs. So's response took me off my feet. She said, "I've watched, as among all nine of us brothers and sisters, that all of you except our brother Chung and I have become Christians. I have seen your lives change. So I do believe your God is true." Wow! I hadn't expected it to come so easily; but her next comment was a letdown. She said, "However, I've worshipped these idols all my life and I don't see any reason why I should change now. I will say that I do believe your God is true." What can you do with that kind of logic? I prayed in my heart for an answer to her.

Then this thought came and with my limited Cantonese I asked her, "Mrs. So, for that first dish you served us, suppose we had said, "We see how your family enjoys it so we really believe it must be good. Because we've never eaten cat or snake before, we don't see any reason why we should try it now; but we really believe it must be good because we see you enjoying it. Would you have believed us?" She smiled and said, "No, not unless you ate it". She got the point.

Martha had grown up in an idol worshipping home so she understood the ins and outs of Buddhism. It was interesting to us Americans to hear one Chinese witness to another. When they seemed to be going in circles, Martha earnestly said to her sister, "This is not something you can just take or leave and it makes no difference. According to God's book, there is an eternal hell waiting for those who refuse Jesus' sacrifice on the cross." Mrs. So replied, "Isn't that a selfish motive for becoming a Christian—to escape hell?" Her logic baffled me.

Having prayed again for an answer, I said, "Mrs. So, I know that first dish you served us cost you a lot of both money and time. You made it very especially for us and we are grateful. Now suppose we had said that it would be selfish of us to eat it all up! How would you have felt? The real issue is not our being selfish in eating it but the insult to you if we had refused it. It cost God a whole lot more in sending His Son to die for us than this dish cost you. Now how does He feel when you refuse the sacrifice of His Son and the gift of eternal life?

We went home with no visible change of heart in Mrs. So. However, her Christian daughter who was my good friend, but absent that night, told me later that her Mom repeated to her these and other illustrations arising from that first dish. Later that week we got a letter from Mrs. So. She requested us to return to help them burn their idols! Two of our missionary gals returned with Martha for this. Mrs. So feared retaliation by the demons during this process so she had their 3-year old grandson stay at some friends' house while, for several hours, they found and destroyed all the idol paraphernalia. After the little tyke who lived with them came back home, he would announce to all their guests, "We've burned our idols and we're worshipping the true God now!" I thought to myself that I would gladly eat bowls of cat and snake if I knew it would bring someone to trust in Jesus. This was a memorable experience for me on my first term in the early '50s; but that was not the end of this story.

THANKS FOR COMING

Now jump ahead some forty years to 1997, just before my retirement from missionary service. By that time our Hong Kong Free churches had multiplied to around 50 churches. They planned a joint all day picnic celebration in a park out near the China border.

Among that crowd a Chinese couple in their 40's came with their children, sought me out and introduced themselves. The father explained. "I was that 3-year old grandson in Mrs. So's house in Macao when you gals came, led my grandma to Jesus, and burned our idols. My grandpa also became a Christian and they were both baptized. So I grew up in a Christian home and now my wife and I are Christians and our children have the blessing of a Christian home. I just want to say, "Thank you for coming".

It was like God's gentle reminder at the close of my ministry that it had not been in vain. His Word would never return void. His anointing on our service will continue to bear fruit and bless others for generations to come, long after my time. I had made the right choice to obey His call, to make my life available to Him.

These are just a sampling of God's faithfulness that I witnessed on my first term in Hong Kong. They were a precursor to greater surprises and blessings that

He had waiting in store for me in the four decades to follow. I've been incredibly blessed.

Chapter 4

AT HOME AND ABROAD

Psalm 90:12-17.

12. Teach us to number our days aright, that we may gain a heart of wisdom. 14. Satisfy us in the morning with your unfailing love that we may sing for joy and be glad all our days.
15. Make us glad for as many days as you have afflicted us, for as many years as we have seen trouble.
16. May your deeds be shown to your servants, your splendor to their children.
17. May the favor of the Lord our God rest upon us; establish thou the work of our hands for us—yes, the work of our hands, establish thou it.

MY FIRST YEAR OF HOME ASSIGNMENT

I had become so involved with those precious Grace Church youth those four years that I felt loath to break away and leave them for my year of home assignment. Since Hong Kong at that time had just one English university and one Chinese University apart from some technical schools or teachers colleges, these students had little chance for further schooling in Hong Kong. Many began to look abroad for college opportunities. When I returned to the United States for that first furlough, I never dreamed that many of those

Grace Church youth so dear to me and who had been so impacted by that revival would eventually come to the United States, too. A number of them settled around the Los Angeles area. They became the nucleus for a church plant that later developed into the present Monterey Park Chinese Evangelical Free Church.

REVERSE CULTURE SHOCK

I had some experiences of culture shock on my first furlough. As I got on the airline bus in Los Angeles, I paid my fare and was about to sit down. The driver barked that I hadn't paid enough. "I gave you a dollar" "You gave me fifty cents, Ma'am!" Oops! My United States fifty cent piece looked just like a Hong Kong dollar! I apologized.

Leaving the Los Angeles airline bus, I tried to cross a busy street as I clutched a suitcase under each arm. Fine! The road was clear or so I thought; but I was looking the wrong direction, the way traffic runs in Hong Kong. I was nearly struck down by a huge flow of traffic bearing down on me! I made it to the center safety aisle and then made the same mistake on the other side. By this time I was unnerved and dripping with sweat as I entered the small hotel where I was booked. I went to my room and looked for drinking water. There was a glass wrapped in cellophane but no pitcher of drinking water. Feeling as if I would die of thirst, I rang for the bell boy. "Here's the glass but where is the drinking water?" I asked him. "The tap, Ma'am, the tap!" He pointed. I had forgotten that you could drink un-boiled tap water here!

A bit unnerved, I decided to go down to the ground floor for a bite to eat. I pressed "G" in the elevator for ground floor and ended up in the garage! I decided to contact some Chinese friends that I knew who lived there. I needed to get back into a culture where I felt at home. I called information for their phone number. The operator said, "Capital 4... "I stopped her. I thought that I was really missing a cog. "Operator, how do you make a capital four?" Oh, no. She burst out laughing. They were using names like Capital back then for the area codes!

TROPICAL MEDICAL TESTS

I returned home to Minneapolis via Chicago where we were supposed to get our arrival physical from Dr. Paul Adolph who was an expert in tropical ailments. I had my appointment to see him on Friday morning; but he told me on the phone that he was leaving town at noon that Friday and wouldn't be back for a week. That was my only chance to see him. I waited that morning for the California Avenue bus as I watched the crowd of people, also waiting, grow larger and larger. I feared that I might never get on that bus even when it would arrive!

Ah, good! I saw a taxi come with its dome light on top. I'd heard taxis are expensive in the United States; but this time, it would be worth it. I dashed out into the street before anyone else got it. I grabbed the rear door handle saying to the driver, "639 North

Central, please. Hey, your rear door is locked!" The driver gave me a big grin and said, "I'm a policeman!" The crowd at the bus stop was smiling too. I wanted to melt and run down the sewer drain. Culture shock! There you have it! I believe God has a sense of humor too.

When I got to Minneapolis to our mission headquarters building, they gave me a mission check in U. S. money for travel. I had another eighty miles to go north by bus or train to my family in Wisconsin. Because it was late Friday afternoon, our mission headquarters had closed their accounts for the week; so no cash was available. "I think you can get the check cashed at Dayton's basement." I did not have enough U. S. money to buy my bus ticket home so I was desperate to get that check cashed. At the Dayton's window I hopefully and fearfully handed over my check. The clerk took a long doubtful look at it and asked, "What denomination?" I replied, hopefully, "Evangelical Free Church." She rolled her eyes and asked, "Do you want fives, tens, or twenties?" I swallowed hard. Obviously she did not care about my church connections!

JOYS OF HOME ASSIGNMENT

My home assignment year was filled with travel and sharing in many churches and homes, especially my burden for the revival at Grace Church and God's marvelous answer to prayer. I met many wonderful Christians back home who took time for a missionary meeting any night of the week! As I shared how God had touched us with revival, many here at home also sought a new touch from God for themselves. My furlough year passed quickly with travel and meetings nearly every night of the week. I calculated that in six months I had slept in ninety beds! I guessed that I'd slept in fresh sheets more often than the Queen of England!

DIVINE APPOINTMENT

While on furlough I experienced some of God's incredible guidance. Here is one example. I was to participate with several other missionaries in a week of "round robin" missionary conferences rotating between three Evangelical Free Churches in three cities – Fargo, North Dakota, Moorhead, Minnesota and Wolverton, Minnesota.

Before this my driving experience had been limited to driving a four-cylinder stick shift Volkswagen Bug around the three square miles of Kowloon, Hong Kong. It was certainly different from home assignment driving. I was handed the keys to a large suburban van with power brakes, power steering and automatic transmission. I feared that if I pressed the wrong dashboard button that I might eject! Clearly I was out of my depth.

I was to stay at a home in Moorhead, then shuttle between services in Moorhead and Fargo for a week. I should finish up the last Sunday in Wolverton which was 20 miles south. I was scheduled to begin speaking that first Sunday morning in Fargo to an 8:30 a.m. adult Sunday school class and the worship service to follow.

I was given a hand drawn map showing me how to take I-90 from Moorhead across the river to Fargo and what I should expect to see along the way. In my ignorance I turned at the first green sign that said "90", unaware that it was **Business 90**! I soon realized that the scenery was not what I had been told to expect. Clearly I was lost and this was before the days of cell phones. There were no gas stations open at 8:00 Sunday morning from which I could call. I knew the class would be waiting for me. I felt so helpless. Going faster in the wrong direction surely would not help; so I stopped the car, got out and prayed for some little old lady to drive by in some little old car that I could safely hail and ask for help. Ah, how quickly God answered prayer. Sure enough, there came a little old lady driving so slowly that I could stop her for help. Did she know where the Evangelical Free Church was? "Not around here," she exclaimed. She opened her passenger door so I could reach across to show her my map which she studied. She gave me very different directions before driving off. Unknown to me, I had left my purse on the front seat of her car! That left me without money, phone numbers or driver's license.

Proceeding according to her directions, I fought an inner battle. I was determined not to panic which was my normal reaction. That would be a victory for the Enemy and a loss of spiritual power for me in my speaking to come. I drove along praising God aloud that

I was His child, His responsibility and I would refuse to worry about being late and lost.

Suddenly when I saw a gas station that was open, I decided to phone the church to assure them that I was coming and to double check my directions. I needed a coin to phone so l hunted around for my purse. Where could it be? I hadn't been any place. I couldn't waste time searching for it. Maybe they'll let me call anyway. Yes, I could use their pay phone. I said that I had no coin because I couldn't find my purse for the pay phone. Could I use their other phone? They said, "No, just continue the direction I was headed and I would find the church. They took me for a cheapskate.

As I pulled into the church yard just a few minutes late, Pastor Dick Hess was out front waiting for me. "Doris, you're late". I answered, "I know. I got lost getting here and I lost my purse doing it!" (I didn't really believe it was lost.) As we ascended the church steps together, he said "Your purse has been found!" I asked, "How could YOU even know it was lost?"

He told how a call came from that little old lady who found a purse on the front seat of her car with chop sticks inside! Could it be from some foreign student? No identification inside. They were in the midst of a family reunion with the whole family trying to solve the mystery of the mysterious purse that appeared in her car. A three year old grandson asked "Granny, did any one come near your car today?" Oh yes! That young lady who was asking directions for the Evangelical Free

Church! She looked up the number and phoned
the church.

My heart melted at God's goodness and care. I
told Pastor Hess that for me to lose my purse was not so
unusual but to find it again: Wow! Maybe this is a
divine appointment; so I asked to accompany Pastor
Hess that afternoon as he went to retrieve my purse.
Was God connecting me to that little old lady?

I sensed a special anointing as I spoke that
morning and I rejoiced that I had not allowed the
Enemy to steal my peace or gain an inroad when I
would have panicked. Although I had no thought nor
mention of raising support that day, one member of that
Sunday school class approached me after class about
wanting to join my team both financially and in prayer.
In fact, he committed to a sizeable chunk of my support
which he fulfilled faithfully until his death years later.
The Lord spoke to my heart, "I was worth trusting,
wasn't I? Because you still trusted me when you were
helpless and lost, I found your purse for you and gave
you a new faithful team partner." The Enemy would
have robbed me of all this by worry.

Pastor Hess drove me to pick up my purse and to
meet again the little old lady who had so helped me. I
noticed her name on the rural mail box as we drove in. I
thanked her for the purse and invited her to my slide
presentation that night at the Free Church. "Oh, no. I
belong to...." and she named another church.

The following Wednesday night I was again involved at the Fargo missionary conference. Now I knew my way but driving back to Moorhead in the dark was harder. Because the city was re-doing the streets, they had taken up all the street signs! Just what I needed! I decided to stop at a gas station ahead that was all lit up to double check my directions. As I got close, I saw it wasn't a gas station at all. It was a Tasty Freeze, all glassed in. I went to the window anyhow to double check my directions. There again I met that same little old lady but this time in Moorhead! She laughed as she recognized me coming again with my directions in hand. Yes, I was headed right. Sorry, the street signs are missing. She invited me inside to meet her daughter and son-in-law who owned this Tasty Freeze. She was helping them to finish up their end-of-the summer season. They were waiting for the closing time of a college event nearby when students would give them some business. I thanked her and went my way. Hmm! Strange to meet that same lady again in another city! "Lord, what do you have up your sleeve in this?"

The next day I heard that the Christian Women's Club was having a luncheon on Friday. Remembering her name on that rural mailbox in Fargo, I looked up her number and I called to invite her as my guest. No, she was too busy helping her daughter to finish the Tasty Freeze season. O.K. Lord. I tried.

On Sunday after giving the morning message at the Wolverton Evangelical Free Church, I was at the door shaking hands with parishioners. One couple looked familiar but I couldn't place them. They said, "Tasty Freeze!" They were the daughter and son-in-law of my "little old lady!" They handed me a $15.00 check for my seminary! Do you go to this church? No, but our daughter does and we come sometimes. I told them that the church would have a potluck supper that evening before the evening service when I would show slides of Hong Kong. They said they'd like to come but they must finish up the Tasty Freeze for the season. Nothing beats a church potluck and this one was no exception. After most folk had finished eating and gone upstairs for the evening service, the Tasty Freeze couple arrived. They had just finished closing down for the season in time to come. They filled their plates and while the husband stood talking with several men, I sat down to visit with the wife as she ate. "So, you come to this church sometimes?" "Yes, our daughter goes here but it is so different here from our church". I had no time for such trivial discussion. The service upstairs was about to begin; so I asked her straight out, "Do you know for sure that you are God's child and on your way to heaven?" Her husband heard this and moved to join us. She replied, "Sometimes I think so and sometimes I'm just not sure." "Would you like to be sure?" "Yes" they both replied. Before that evening service began, both husband and wife prayed trusting Christ as their Lord and Savior, becoming God's children and later faithful members of that church.

This was the divine appointment that God was leading me to, with such unexpected means by allowing me to get lost on my way to a meeting, by allowing me to leave my purse in a stranger's car, by letting me mistake a Tasty Freeze for a gas station, etc., and by stretching my faith. Surely this God is worth trusting! He bears with our goofs and turns our boo-boos into blessings. Oh, what a God we serve!

MATCHMAKING

Thankfully, furlough also left some time to spend with my family on the farm and my brother in Minneapolis. Before I ever left for the field, between my college graduation in June and sailing for Hong Kong in September, I had done a little matchmaking – for my brother. I had arranged for a dear Wheaton classmate, Jean Krager, to come to our home farm in Wisconsin for a week. I chose my brother's vacation week "so we could use his car"! That matchmaking effort paid off. By my first furlough four years later, my brother and this dear classmate were married, had a year-old son, and I had a place to stay when I was in the Twin Cities where our headquarters were located.

Psalm 8: 1, 3-4.
1. O Lord, our Lord, how excellent is thy name in all the earth! Who has set thy glory above the heavens.
3. When I consider thy heavens, the work of thy fingers, the moon and the stars, which thou hast ordained;
4. What is man, that thou are mindful of him? And the son of man, that thou visiteth him?

BRIEF NEW TERM

When I went back to the field for my second term, I prayed for God to lead me into a ministry that was right for me. I never dreamed that it would be in literature. That sounded boring to me. I was told that the market in Hong Kong for children's literature was flooded with risqué material. Rows of young kids who had paid a few cents to pour over those corrupting paperbacks would sit along the street. Our local Free Church literature board began producing a very attractive evangelistic children's monthly magazine. We would have to produce it in quantity to meet the costs; but we found it hard to interest enough church parents into subscribing to it. The children loved it but they had no money. Every month the magazine ran further into debt. Finally, at one literature board meeting, it was moved to terminate the magazine due to the low subscriptions and high costs. I pleaded for and won a one month reprieve in shutting down the magazine. We prayed together and individually for some breakthrough within the following month and for some better way to distribute it.

SUBSCRIPTION BREAKTHROUGH

With this burden heavy on my heart, the next week I was driving my Volkswagen bug down "Wash Clothes Street" in Kowloon and noticed a large elementary school. On an impulse I parked up on the sidewalk, walked in and asked some cleaning ladies for the name of the school principal. When I was ushered into his office, I spoke with him about the evil material that the children were reading on the streets. He agreed and was very concerned himself. I told him our mission was doing something about it, and I showed him several back issues of our Children's Friend Magazine. Just off the cuff and without any preplanning, I offered myself as available to return to speak to his student assembly to tell the children an uplifting compelling story like they might find in the magazine. This was a novelty to him to have a Cantonese-speaking Westerner come to speak at his assembly so he immediately agreed. I was invited. It became an unplanned "God thing".

The timing of this was just after the Chinese New Year when all Chinese children get red lucky-money envelopes from all their married relatives. It was the one time of the year that the kids would likely have money to spend. I returned to their school assembly a week later with a stack of subscription blanks with our most attractive recent magazine cover picture on the front, plus a subscription blank and a letter of explanation to their parents on the back. When I spoke to the assembly, I told the children a typical story like they might find in that magazine which included the gospel. I promised to return in a week to collect
their subscriptions.

"LUCKY MONEY"

With the aid of their recent Chinese New Year's "lucky money", subscriptions poured in. "Hey, thanks, Lord. This method really works". I began to go from school to school using this approach and speaking in many school assemblies each week. It was a great open door to clearly give out the Gospel as well as collect subscriptions to the Children's Friend Magazine where the children would continue to get the Gospel each month. With the help of my 4-cyclinder, stick shift Volkswagen Bug, which was a gift from my uncle, I was able to get around to speak in many school assemblies—up to five school assemblies a day! God had answered our prayers by giving us a new way to publicize this magazine as well as share the Gospel to thousands of children in many schools. Because Hong Kong was under British rule and these were mostly private schools, the religious emphasis was not a problem.

Subscriptions grew to over 4,000. Instead of the Children's Friend Magazine being discontinued back then in the 50's, this magazine has continued reaching children for Christ for over 50 years. Many salvation decisions have resulted. Some of our seminary students plus pastors serving in Hong Kong today have testified that their first introduction to the Gospel was through that little magazine! God surely answered our prayers.

LITERATURE MINISTRY CLOSED

I had just been back on the field a year and a half from home assignment and well launched into the literature ministry when suddenly a rug seemed pulled out from under me. I had felt so blessed by the opportunities to share the Gospel in Cantonese in so many schools to so many children. Furthermore, the

Children's Friend Magazine, instead of being discontinued, was set to continue its ministry for another fifty years! I thought I had found my niche. Suddenly God apparently had other plans for me. "Would I be available?"

HOSPITAL MINISTRY

I had been struggling to keep up this pace in spite of a growing weakness and running chronic unexplained fevers. Finally I landed in a large government hospital where blood tests verified that I had Undulant Fever from drinking unpasteurized goats' milk from a goat with Bang's disease. My treatment required 17 days in the government hospital.

I shared my hospital room with a well-educated Chinese Catholic lady. The priest came regularly to offer her Mass. She had been both a nurse and a secretary in the war. Her husband had been a fighter pilot. One day after a plane crash she and some other nurses had to go to collect what body parts they could find from the crash. Afterwards she was given a list of the passengers' names to type up. One was her husband!

We became good friends and I shared the Gospel with her. She commented, "You Protestants are lucky. You can read the Bible yourselves. We only get what the priest says". She was still a loyal Catholic. I told her there is a Catholic version of the New Testament which is in more modern English and has the Pope's statement in it that Catholics can read it. It is the Confraternity New Testament. I promised her that if I got out of the hospital before she did, I would go to the Catholic bookstore and buy her one. I did and she took it as if it had been gold. She had a deep spiritual hunger.

Two weeks later I returned to the hospital to get the verdict on my case. I first visited my Catholic friend and she had almost completed reading her New Testament! Her heart was ripe. She prayed to receive Christ and trust in HIS righteousness instead of her own.

SENT HOME

The doctor told me that they have only one treatment for Undulant Fever. They had tried it on me but my body had not responded. "How long will it take you to pack up your stuff and return to the States?" I asked for a prognosis for when I could expect to return to Hong Kong? He answered "possibly in one year, or ten years or never!" "The medication did not work for you." Bewildered, I went home to pack.

I had prayed for healing. Surely God could heal me; but God gave me a verse from James in the Amplified New Testament, "*Expect and patiently wait for the mercy of the Lord your God upon you*". It would have been His mercy to heal me; but "*Expect and patiently wait*". Okay, Lord, I'll wait. A large box of fruit was delivered to my door with a note from that Catholic lady. She thanked me for those days that I shared with her in the hospital that had led her to a personal relationship with the Lord. Okay, Lord, you had a purpose for me being there and I believe you have a purpose in sending me back home! The Children's Friend Magazine continued to grow in my absence as Chinese coworkers continued my method of visiting schools and introducing the magazine.

EMERGENCY BACK HOME

I arrived back to my Wisconsin home on a Saturday night in January, 1960. My brother, his wife and son came up from Minneapolis for a happy family reunion. The next morning before church, Dad had suspicious symptoms so my brother took him into town to see the doctor. It was a heart attack! Although my brother had to return to his job in the city, I was available to help Mom with the barn chores and I could take her the 9-mile drive to visit Dad in the hospital because she didn't drive. The snow was deep and I was there to shovel paths to the barn and woodpile. I realized how God had brought me all that way home to be present at this family emergency. "Expect and patiently wait."

That week my mom got the flu. I had her come to the barn to sit on a stool and teach me the individual formula to feed each of the calves. I did the milking and then took her into town to the doctor. He said, "She has the flu. We'll keep her in the hospital for three days and she will be fine." What a blessing that I could do the chores in her place. She ate a good hospital supper that evening; but when the nurse came to get her dinner tray, she was gone! It was her heart. Now she went to heaven on a full stomach. *"Patiently wait for the mercy of the Lord your God upon you"*. How tender the Lord was to bring me home for such a time.

Actually, it was two years before I could return to Hong Kong. I was home to care for my dad on his slow recovery and the repeated hospitalizations. Dad wanted to die rather than to keep me from returning to the mission field. By the notes under his hospital tray cloth, Dad courted the hospital cook—a widowed lady and family friend from years back. She was 12 years younger than Dad. She told me, "I can care for your dad so you can return to the mission field." She did this as her service to the Lord. Dad could just stand up long enough for the marriage ceremony that was conducted at home in our living room and then he had to lie down again. She nursed him back to health and God gave them twelve very happy years together. One month after their wedding, she was to become the hostess to thirty Chinese students!

A FARM REUNION!

Before leaving Hong Kong, I had been working with a large youth group of some 70 young people from our Grace Evangelical Free Church and was awed to see God bring to them a spiritual revival that totally transformed that high school group. Let me hasten to add that this work of God was quite apart from me because my Cantonese was still very limited. I had been in their homes and eaten at their tables; but I never dreamed that one day they could come to MY home in Wisconsin!

These dear students were soon scattered in colleges from California and Texas to the east coast; but they conspired together and wrote to me, asking if they could come to our Wisconsin farm for a reunion—a 3-day gathering together for fellowship and spiritual uplift before the start of their fall college term. Actually 30 of them came in cars that they had pooled their resources to buy for less than 100 dollars each for that trip!!

My preparation was to buy wall-board from the local lumber yard and single-handedly finish our heretofore unfinished "A-frame" attic store-room so over a dozen girls could sleep in a finished attic on the floor on mattresses borrowed from a camp. The boys slept in the haymow on fresh new hay. One fellow commented, "The crickets jumped from one face to another." They made Chinese food in our small kitchen from our abundant September garden. It was served on doors placed across sawhorses for tables in the yard. On the night before their arrival, I had pulled in a full bucket of fresh fish from a nearby lake.

My father, still recovering from his January heart attack, and just newly remarried, was overjoyed to see again and host so many Chinese Christian youth!

Our worship services were held in our granary, where all 30 of us sat on borrowed benches with straw covering the floor. Our setting was such a contrast to our speaker, Dr. Voget, a very dignified, sophisticated lady professor from Wheaton College! She was my favorite teacher who, in my college days, had really deepened my own spiritual life. She touched their lives too.

On Sunday these Chinese students gave my home church an unforgettable testimony service. This church had prayed so much for these youth and now they had the fruit of their prayers stand before them as they praised God! This experience was perhaps unique in mission history! The blessing was simply overwhelming to us all. Only God could have orchestrated this. His fantastic and mysterious ways!!

Chapter 5

REFLECTIONS ON GOD'S MYSTERIOUS WAYS

HOW GOD SPEAKS

I think you will agree that God speaks to us today primarily by three methods: 1) through Creation, 2) through Scripture and 3) through Testimonies.

This is an example through creation: My father told of a time that he was driving his 1927 Chevy touring car in Inner Mongolia along the edge of the Gobi Desert, far from civilization, when his car stalled and would go no further. As Dad got out to check on the problem, he had a surprising encounter with a hermit who lived there alone. Before checking the car, Dad visited with that hermit. What was he living out there for? The hermit was searching for the Spirit Being who must have made the world and all of nature. Dad was overjoyed to share with him the good news of the true God who not only created the world but also provided a way for us to become His child and enjoy His presence forever!

The hermit who had observed God in nature said, "All my life I have been waiting for what I have heard today. Now I can die in peace." According to Romans

1:20: *"the invisible things of Him from the creation of the world are clearly seen, even His eternal power and Godhead, being understood by the things that are made"*.

Yes, God does speak through nature but it is an incomplete revelation. After leading that hermit to Christ, Dad's car started up fine! That whole surprising episode was just one example of "God's mysterious ways."

Secondly, God speaks to us today through scripture. This is the most complete revelation of God. In scripture, we learn much about God's will and character through His dealings with men of long ago.

Thirdly, God speaks to us through His dealings with people today. This is through the testimonies of how He is at work in lives all around us, sometimes in unexpected, surprising and even humorous ways.

It is through this third method that I pray God will speak to us now as I share with you some simple stories of how I have seen Him at work in Hong Kong.

Isaiah 55:8-9

For my thoughts are not your thoughts, neither are your ways my ways, saith the Lord. For as the heavens are higher than the earth, so are my ways higher than your ways, and my thoughts than your thoughts.

I was to learn this over and over in my 44 years of ministry in Hong Kong—1953-1997.

MINISTRY PRINCIPLES

Fortunately, before I ever went to Hong Kong, God had taught me several valuable principles.

One such principle impacted me one night during my last semester at Wheaton College when I hoped to sail for Hong Kong in a few months. That night I was walking alone back to the dorm after supper. The air was perfectly still as huge flat snowflakes floated silently down and absorbed all sound. That incredibly beautiful scene of the snowflakes against the old fashioned street lamps remains with me today.

The background for that was an inner struggle that I'd been having because I was feeling so inwardly unprepared for the mission field. How could I go to Hong Kong and tell a drug addict that God could change his habits when I still struggled with my temper and impatience? While I was absorbing that magical snow scene, God's Spirit brought to mind a number of helpful Scriptures that I had memorized.

Col 1:25-27

The mystery of the Gospel that which sets it apart from all other religion, is that God is not just some Spirit Being out there we can call on for help. The great mystery is CHRIST IN YOU, the hope of glory.

Col 2:9
In Christ was all the fullness of the Godhead bodily and I am complete in Him!

All God's power abides in Christ and Christ lives in me by His Spirit. That means that I have all the resources that I need as long as I am depending on Him and not on my own smarts! It was a magical moment that I'll never forget as I walked through that beautiful scene, singing softly to myself, "Christ liveth in me, Christ liveth in me, Oh, what a salvation this, that Christ liveth in me". (Christ Liveth In Me. Words by Daniel W. Whittle and Music by James McGranahan.) In that magical moment, He had assured me that all the resources I needed were mine.

Another vital principle was: it is not our working FOR God that counts, but His working THROUGH us. When we try to work FOR God, we are simply being busy, spinning our wheels. Wood, hay and stubble result. When we trust _Him_ to do _His_ work _through_ us, He often does remarkable things beyond our expectations. Then HE gets the glory.

The first missionaries in Acts had this principle straight in Acts 14:26. When the disciples returned from their first missionary journey to their sending church in Antioch, they reported not on what they had done <u>FOR</u> God, but *"all that God had done THROUGH them"*. And in Acts 15:4 at their great church council, they again reported *"all that God had done <u>THROUGH</u> them"*.

That is the same kind of report I want to leave with you here. Not MY work FOR God, but of HIS work in the lives that I have seen Him work and often in unexpected ways.

RETURN TO HONG KONG

After two years in the States, I was overjoyed to hear the doctor pronounce my illness to be in remission so I could return to Hong Kong to continue my ministry. I wondered what God had up His sleeve for me this time? I was burdened to work with youth although I had never been able to fit a "youth work" course into my study schedule. As before, I would simply have to depend on God!

My fellow missionaries had rented for me an upper middle class fifth floor apartment, one of four such apartments on each floor. I wondered about my neighbors. What would be the best way to meet them? Would I have any ministry in this building? Were there children for a weekly Bible story time? Were there any youth? How would I get acquainted? I breathed a prayer for this.

I would be living close to our "Mission Home" which was a three story building that was built by our mission for missionary families. It had a grass lawn plus a large garage that was converted into a sealed dry storage space for household items of furloughing missionaries. With Hong Kong's high humidity, a dehydrated dry place to store your stuff while on home assignment was invaluable. Other than the furniture that I had parceled out for others to use in my absence, all of my stuff as well as that of other furloughing missionaries was stashed in there. The men of our mission would help me move my stuff out; but not until "next week" when they'd have time. Since my assigned apartment was just a few buildings down from this mission home, I got a bright idea.

Being too impatient to wait for the men's help, I recruited our missionary kids to use one of their wagons and help me to move a lot of stuff that first day, including my fold-up metal army cot with its straw-stuffed mattress. The kids were delighted to help. By the end of the day after so much moving, I was too tired to even unfold and make up my cot so I planned to sleep on the mattress on the floor. I emptied my coat pockets of all the keys that I'd been given that day and dumped them all on the dresser.

Oops! I had forgotten to get back my dog, Bop Eye, from the family who had been keeping her for me. Fellow missionaries had told me that it was not safe for me to stay there alone overnight without my dog or my roommate who was coming later. Although it was late, I dashed out in a hurry to go for my dog. I forgot that my keys were all on the dresser! Once the door slammed, I couldn't get back in and now my stuff was there and not safe either. Because men are supposed to solve everything, I walked back to the mission home for help. "We gave you all the keys this morning!" Efforts by Don Carlson to break in with a kitchen knife proved futile; so from the Carlson's flat in desperation, I called the fire department and described my emergency situation. They responded positively. Yes, they could come with a ladder and let me in. "On one condition", I said, "No sirens, please". "At your request, madam, there will be no sirens; but you better get back there to show us where to go." It was now after 11:00 p.m. and all the lights in my building were out.

MEETING MY NEIGHBORS

Suddenly I heard a siren. No! It can't be! A fire truck was coming around the corner and up our street with its siren blaring full blast. A second fire truck, a chemical truck and an ambulance, as for a full 5-alarm fire, all stopped in front of my building! The frightened residents awoke and poured out of my building like ants. Did I pray to meet my neighbors? Oh, I met them all right! All on the first night! That prayer was quickly answered. Ah, God's unexpected, unique and humbling answer to my prayer!

The firemen jumped off the fire trucks with their hoses, "Where's the fire?" I had to explain that I had locked myself out! With my pajama-dressed neighbors watching from the ground below, the fire chief entered the flat above mine, hooked the smallest fireman by the belt and let him down over the wall from the sixth floor balcony to my balcony where he could enter my flat.

Then the fire chief turned to me. "Now prove to me that this is your flat. The last time we let someone in, we found later that we had let a thief in who robbed the place!" The folded army cot and straw mattress on the floor were proof enough! Ah, yes, I had quickly met all my neighbors and a weekly children's Bible story time did follow; but God had another reason for putting me there. It was to reach a key person for Him in that building.

Julie, a high school girl, lived in one of the apartments on my floor. I wanted to make friends with her but both she and her family seemed afraid of me. If she saw me in the hall, she'd scoot back indoors faster than a cockroach under light. She knew me from that first night but she wouldn't warm up.

MY FAILED PROMISE

Within that next year, Billy Graham was scheduled to hold a one night evangelistic meeting in Hong Kong's largest stadium across the harbor. It was well advertised. Some of Julie's classmates planned to attend so she was curious. I happened to catch her in the hall and invited her to the meeting. To my surprise she agreed to go with me! I was delighted.

I had invited so many people to that service. They would fill both my little Volkswagen Bug plus two taxis that I had hired to follow me to pick up everyone for whom I had promised rides. Picking all these people up would take quite some time so I suggested that Julie wait at home and I would pick her up last, rather than have her ride around so long in the heat.

Can you believe it? With all the excitement of gathering all those people, I totally forgot about Julie! However, God didn't forget her. She waited until the last minute and still I hadn't come. Several of her classmates came by to ask her to go there with them. Alas, she said no. She was waiting for Hui Kwoo Neung (my name) to come for her.

After that service, as the arena and seats cleared, here came Julie down the aisle, smiling with arms outstretched. Her first words were "Tonight I trusted Jesus!" My heart sank. "How did you get here?" "By taxi!" After waiting for me so long, she had hired a taxi to reach the stadium by herself! I was both chagrined and dumbfounded. God had saved her that night, not *because* of me but *in spite* of me! His ways surely are higher than our ways.

Julie and I became good friends; but her parents forbad her to attend church. I emphasized that as a Christian she must obey her parents. Because church was off limits, I arranged individual Bible studies for her every week but not in church. She memorized Scripture, read her Bible, grew as a Christian and was very much in love with Jesus. After many months her parents relented and allowed her to attend church and youth fellowship where she blossomed as a Christian. Her obedience at home won her freedom. Eventually, Julie finished high school and went on to Milwaukee to college. Her mother, who had been so antagonistic, followed her to the United States where Julie led her mother to Jesus before her death. Today Julie is married to a godly Chinese pharmacist. They have a Christian home and are <u>pillars</u> in a Chinese Baptist church of Fort Worth, Texas. Julie the girl that I first met due to a fire engine siren and then forgot to pick up for a Graham crusade! Surely God's ways are higher than ours!

AN INVITATION TO YOUTH WORK

After my recovery and returning to Hong Kong for this new term, I prayed for guidance about where to serve. During my previous brief term, before illness sent me home, I had worked with literature distribution. What was God's plan for me now? I was available and searching.

Very soon an invitation letter came from our Living Springs Free Church asking me to work with their young people. I visited the next Saturday afternoon's youth meeting. Just six teenagers showed up even though this was the welcome service for juniors just being promoted to join the regular youth group! A total of just six? Again the next Saturday there were just six but not the SAME six. Lord, how can you build anything with this? It was not much to work with.

I prayed about their invitation letter and surprisingly felt at peace in accepting although the situation looked pretty hopeless. Besides the church was far from where I lived.

My uncle had given me in U.S. currency $7,000.00 the cost of a new 4-cylinder stick shift Volkswagen Bug which I used to do a lot of visitation to get to know those kids. The whole Living Springs Church was not much more than a tiny enclosed corner-balcony overhang above the street. It was on the second story of a 12 story old building. No elevator! It had narrow steps and little space; so the church rented a classroom of a school that met next door in the same building. There I began teaching a teenage Sunday School class on Sunday mornings. Attendance was sparse and irregular.

These were good kids and I sought to see some evidence of spiritual life among them. Had any of them really been born again and were they enjoying fellowship with God? I couldn't tell. Peter, one of our active teens, and his family with younger sisters lived a few stories above the church so I visited them often. Samuel was another active teen who lived high up in a building nearby. His dad had four wives and he claimed 28 siblings! Some had grown and left the nest but they were still a huge family. With no place for him to sleep, Samuel became our church watchman. At night he slept in our church on our hard benches.

Water rationing made life difficult in those days. We had water in our tap for just a few hours on every fourth day! You washed clothes and stored water for drinking, washing, bathing and the bathroom until your next water day. It was hot and humid. Every family member took turns daily, bathing in the same bathtub of dirty water for three days. The floors of those old buildings couldn't support the storage of much water either. I learned a lot about the home backgrounds and trials of those kids as I spent time with them.

I remembered the advice by an old pastor to me in my Bible School days when I spent a summer of internship down in the hills of Kentucky. He said, "When you get to the mission field, Doris, you will find plenty of other Western missionaries to socialize with and they speak your language; but the Chinese will be watching you to see with whom you choose to spend your leisure time. By this they will see whether they are your work or your friends!" That made a deep impression on me. I did not believe in keeping "office hours" because I couldn't imagine the Apostle Paul doing that. Like him I was free of family responsibilities.

Aside from my daily time with the Lord, daily language study, message or lesson preparation, mission meetings, etc., when those kids were free I made sure that I was available to them and poured my life into them. However, life transformation did not happen easily.

A MOVE TO NEW QUARTERS

Eventually Peter's family, who had lived a few floors above the church, moved to a newly finished 15 story apartment building that was just a few blocks from the church, with an elevator and many apartments on each floor. With Peter's urging and wanting to get closer to our church, I moved there into an eleventh floor flat in this very Chinese-style fairly new apartment building. On the two lowest floors in my building was a giant Chinese department store! Often the elevators didn't work and I'd really regret it if I'd forgotten something important such as my car keys back in my eleventh floor flat! Climb eleven stories in the heat? Ufta! One day when I boarded the elevator which wasn't working right and descending at an exasperating pace, there were two little boys already on board. When I got on, one said solemnly to the other in Chinese, not knowing that I'd understand, "We'll go down faster now that SHE got on!"

Peter's family's apartment was a few stories down from mine. He had a tank of tropical fish and so did I, primarily for a point of contact. Tropical fish were cheap and beautiful and we had this common interest. Our city water was chlorinated so we'd have to draw a bucket of water the night before to let the chlorine evaporate before we changed our fish tank water. One night I saved water for this. The next morning I cleaned my tank to give them fresh water. They swam so lively that I thought they were delighted with the fresh water; but I was wrong. They began going belly up. I phoned down to Peter. "My fish are dying from the fresh water that I gave them. The chlorine must not all have evaporated. Do you have any evaporated water on hand?" "No", he said, "but you can bring yours down and put your still live ones into my tank." I did but I didn't think to take out the dead ones first! A terrible cultural blunder!

His parents stayed polite until I left; then they lit into Peter for getting involved with church and that 'foreign devil' missionary lady (me) who was now bringing tragedy into their home. Their family had plans to immigrate to Canada. Now I had brought death into their home. Not only would they never get to Canada but someone in their family would die! Wouldn't you know it! That next day Peter's bike was stolen at school! "See, what did we tell you? All kinds of disasters are coming to our family because of that missionary lady." It got so tough for Peter at home that one night he didn't go home. He went instead to our church to spend a night like Samuel and to sleep on a church bench. His mom figured out where he was and went to the church to drag him home. That was her first and only time to enter our church. Peter was too polite to tell me about the trouble I had brought him.

Finally, Samuel told me about Peter's problems at home. They were because I had brought dead fish into their home. I recruited a lot of prayer support; then I went to Peter's flat to apologize to his folks. I admitted my ignorance of their belief that bringing dead fish into their home would bring them death. I said that I wouldn't belittle their fear of the evil spirits and Satan's power that could harm them. Satan's power is real. My whole reason for coming to Hong Kong was to bring the good news that Jesus came and He overcame the power of Satan. We need not fear him anymore. I had a wonderful open door to share the Gospel and Jesus' victory with them. They really listened. After my apology I returned to my flat. That evening they sent their youngest daughter up to my flat to invite me to dinner in their home the next night. That meant I was forgiven.

NEW NEIGHBORS IN A NEW BUILDING

When I moved into Peter's building, I wondered what ministry I might have there. How would I meet my neighbors this time? My apartment was long and narrow with windows and light only on one narrow end. Since there was no yard for hanging my wash, I had nailed two pair of notched boards high on the opposite walls of my bedroom to hold two bamboo poles. I could hang any number of bamboo poles across them to hang up my washing to dry. I washed my clothes in a small tub with a motor in the cover which turned an agitator for washing. I rinsed and wrung them out by hand; so I had an upside down dripping rain forest in my bedroom hanging from the bamboo poles every time I washed clothes. My wash never saw the sun.

I had two pink sheets for my army cot. I wanted just for once to hang them in the sun; so I hooked wire loops over the open-out window handles to hold the ends of a long bamboo pole. I would hang my sheets over that pole to dry and hope they wouldn't get blown against the dirty building. Pleased with my success, I went to collect the now dry sheets. Just as I had unclipped the clothes pins holding the sheets on the pole, a gentle breeze lifted one sheet from my bamboo pole and sent it high out over the street like a flying carpet. I looked down eleven stories at the street below with its six lanes of traffic. I could imagine one of my sheets enveloping a car below and causing a terrible accident. I was the only Westerner within blocks and on each sheet was clearly written my name, "Doris Ekblad".

As I gazed in horror and even before I had time for an SOS prayer, another breeze blew the sheet back and it got caught on someone's opened-out window below. I tried to count how many stories down from mine. That didn't work; so I took the elevator down and tried to count up from below. Again I was too close to count. I went to the next intersection where I could cross the street and there I counted how many floors up and which apartment across where I could find my pink sheet. When I had figured out which apartment, taken the elevator, and knocked on that unit's door, the couple who lived there were shocked to see a Westerner at all in their building and even more so to hear me speak Cantonese! When I asked, "Would you please check your windows to see if my pink sheet is caught on your windows?" They burst out laughing. Sure enough, there was my sheet hung up on their window. They invited me in to drink tea with them and gave permission for their junior-aged son to begin attending our Sunday School and junior youth group. This boy came faithfully and rounded up many other kids in the building for my weekly Bible story time with them in my flat. There was a seed sowing opportunity there and one key kid reached, all because of my pink flying carpet! Again I could never have dreamed up such a way to meet my new neighbors. Surely, God's ways, as He said, are higher than our ways!!

ROOF TOP POWER

With people spilling out of the high rise buildings all around our church, it made no sense that we were ministering to so few young people. I was not satisfied. I saw little sign of spiritual life in the few kids that we had. I was really burdened for them. I persuaded our building watchman to give me a key to our roof. That was not easily granted because they were afraid of suicides.

It was good for me to get out from the tight squeeze and congestion of where I lived and the high buildings all around me. I wondered how many hundred people there were living just in my 15-story building alone! On that roof I was able to get out from under it all as I overlooked the beautiful harbor and prayed for those kids for long periods of time each day. I prayed for God to work in their lives and to bring more youth into the hearing of the Gospel. The times of prayer up there lifted my spirits as I worshipped my Lord and shared His heart for those kids. It was an important part of each day. I also shared this prayer request with faithful prayer partners back home. I believe their prayer backing was one secret behind what God was preparing to do with that youth group. It was a work that continues to this day and beyond what I could have asked or dreamed.

YOUTH WORK PRINCIPLES

As I prayed, God laid on my heart two principles or goals to work by:

1. Jesus Christ must become the chief attraction in our youth fellowship, not games or eats or outings or socials, but Jesus Christ himself the visibly chief attraction to our group. Then we would draw the kids who had a spiritual hunger.
2. We would aim for quality rather than quantity. "Lord, give us not just numbers but a nucleus of kids who will be totally committed to follow and obey you at any cost." I prayed first for a nucleus of ONE such teen.

NUCLEUS BEGUN

I began to notice one girl, Gloria, who started coming to the youth fellowship very regularly and on time too. I went to visit her and shared with her the burden on my heart for those kids and my prayer for a nucleus of ONE who was totally committed to Jesus Christ. She replied, "I want that." We prayed together as she gave her whole life over to God. I began to disciple her with verses to memorize, a Bible correspondence course, etc. I rejoiced in her spiritual growth. I would take her along in my Volkswagen Bug as I went to visit the other kids.

First we would pray together in my car for the kids. Often we never got farther than my car as the burden to pray came upon her, too. As we just kept praying, it got too late to visit anybody!

While I was rejoicing at this first answer to my prayer for a nucleus of one, I suddenly got bad news. Gloria's whole family was emigrating to Texas! Gloria was about 15 or 16, and the only Christian in her family. She knew hardly any English. What would become of her spiritually in Texas? God, what are you doing? You are making a mistake! Gloria is the beginning answer to my prayer and you are snatching her away? Do I start all over? I was devastated.

When the fellows in our youth group heard the news that she was leaving, a number of our guys fell madly in love with her. Puppy love of course. They hadn't started dating and now they couldn't have her because she was leaving. The boys cried so at the airport. Gloria, in her quiet way had shaped the image for our teen-aged guys for what kind of a girl they wanted in their future. A God-fearing girl like Gloria!

Three years later when I returned to the United States for furlough, I routed my flight through San Antonio, Texas, to see Gloria. I found her to be a spiritual leader in the large Chinese church youth group there with many coming to her for counsel. The music minister of that Chinese church eventually married her and their family has been greatly used of God ever since. Whenever I go to Texas to visit family, I visit Gloria and speak in her Chinese church! God had other plans for our Living Springs Church youth group and He didn't need Gloria to do it. He had work for her in Texas.

ANSWERED PRAYER FOR LIVING SPRINGS

That fall our united FCYF (Free Church Youth Fellowship) from our seven churches was planning a united youth conference. These conferences had been deeply spiritual in the past. Unfortunately few of our Living Springs youth had attended. I thought, if only we could get our kids to this conference where they'd hear the Word and see other youth their age who were really alive for God and in love with Jesus, that could turn their lives around; but at Living Springs we still had just a rotating handful of kids each week at our youth meetings. Oh, they'd planned and led their own meetings. It was interesting enough and good leadership training but any social club could have done that. The spiritual dimension was hardly visible and our numbers stayed few.

I suggested we dig up old Sunday School records of any children that had ever attended our Sunday School in years past. They'd be teens by now. Let's get their addresses, visit them and invite them to the youth conference. Yeah, our core group and I made a lot of contacts. We had to first persuade these teens to WANT to come to the conference, persuade their parents to <u>let</u> them come and then pay half of their way. After a summer of such work, we ended up with 18 teens with at least some past connection with Living Springs who were committed to attend this conference! I was overjoyed. I had prayed so much for these kids. Now I had high expectations of God using this conference to transform their lives.

Unfortunately, back when I didn't expect any of our youth to attend, I had promised to speak that same week to our primary kids' camp in another part of the city! Bummer! I wanted to be with our Living Springs youth. Too late! I did promise them that on Friday afternoon, when my responsibilities were finished at the primary-age camp, I would drive out to their youth conference in the New Territory beyond the city and be with them for their last night.

CONFERENCE RESULTS

When I arrived on that Friday afternoon, our Living Springs youth were all gathered at the campgrounds to welcome me and all talking at once. They wanted me to go and pick "dragon-eyes" with them. It was a type of fruit (I don't know the real English name). I asked them, "Have you guys gotten much out of this week?" Samuel said, "Oh, the basketball has been great and I got by with just 2 minutes of talking with my counselor". He did not care for any interview about his spiritual life! One girl said, "Oh, the boys have been naughty." Really, what did they do? "Oh, they were chewing gum in the meetings!" My heart sank. Did anything of significance happen in their lives this week? I turned to John who was chairman of our youth group. "John, did you get anything out of this week?" He knew what I meant and he shook his head. I asked, "John, do you want help?" He nodded so I walked off with him.

The group who were insensitive to what was going on groaned. "Oh, we wanted to pick dragon-eyes with you."

I asked John, our chairman, "Are you really a Christian?" He said, "No, I could never be a real Christian. You have no idea what temptations I face." I said, "John, if you'll invite Jesus into your life, He'll give you strength from the INSIDE." He shook his head; then I said, "John, if you'll give your life to Christ, I'll commit to giving you individual time each week to help you grow." With that encouragement he bowed his head and prayed to receive Christ. When he finished praying, he turned to me and said, "Don't expect a testimony from me tonight!" That was the last night of our conference and it was scheduled for testimonies.

There were so many heartwarming testimonies that night; but none from our 18 Living Springs youth. I was nearly in tears. I had prayed so much for this week and counted on God to use it to change lives. That was MY way but not God's way.

On Saturday morning we returned to the city by hired buses which were full of joyous youth singing all the way. Their tagged luggage would be dropped off by truck at each church they came from to be picked up by the kids that evening. The youth of each church had scheduled their own testimony meeting for that Saturday night. I murmured to myself. Yeah, what kind of testimonies will we have at Living Springs? We got the kids to the conference but their hearts were not prepared so they got nothing out of it. So much wasted energy! I was in for a surprise.

SATURDAY BREAKTHROUGH

Strangely, on that Saturday a very sudden and unexpected typhoon blew up. I've never seen one come so suddenly and fast. Street signs were flying in the gusts. The parents told their kids, "You can't go out tonight. It's dangerous." The kids insisted that they'd have to go to the church to get their suitcases and clothes. In those days they might have had only one change of clothes.

Unbelievably, twelve kids showed up that night for youth fellowship. They nearly doubled our usual attendance and they risked a raging typhoon to get there. The first testimony was from Samuel, the kid who got by with just 2 minutes talking with his counselor. "Oh, I had fun this week. The basketball was terrific; but it was not until last night, when I heard the testimonies of the kids from our other churches, that I realized what I'd missed. I wish you guys would pray for me that when God is blessing the other kids, He won't pass me by." This set the tone for our whole evening with one after another asking for prayer and spiritual reality. We ended up on our knees with a never-to-be forgotten prayer meeting that turned their lives and that whole youth group around. Every one of their lives was touched. When we finally finished praying, we listened to the radio news. A number ten top typhoon signal was up so no one could go out or go home. Since they had their week's luggage at the church, we just pulled the curtains for the Sunday School rooms and we all slept on the hard church benches for the night.

DEEPER SHARING

On Sunday morning after early individual Quiet-Time, the first for many, someone suggested, "Let's each share what God has spoken to us about this morning from our Quiet-Time. It became a weekly practice to come early, long before Sunday School time, to share together their struggles and victories plus nuggets from the Word from that week. They were very honest. "I blew up at my Mom this week." "I got mad at my little sis and tore up her school notebook," etc.; then they prayed for each other. It was a very precious and open fellowship.

I thought, now God, I'd have expected you to use normal means to answer my prayers for those kids like Gloria's influence or that conference to wake those kids up spiritually. Instead, God, you used a raging typhoon and a prayer meeting, AFTER the conference, on a night when no one should even have been out! Surely, Your ways are higher than my ways.

The youth began to request of me training workshops on how to study the Bible, how to lead Bible studies, how to share their faith with their classmates and how to start a prayer group among other Christian kids at their school. They needed basic Bible doctrine to protect them from cults.

MORMONS

One cult sending missionaries to Hong Kong was the Mormons. They visited homes door to door, attracting young people and building their beautiful churches. Our youth decided that they should study up on the Mormon heresy and schedule one Saturday night meeting to sharing their discoveries and how to reach out to the Mormons. One Sunday afternoon when I came home from church, I found the Mormons combing my building. I figured on another hour before they'd reach my unit so I got on the phone and called as many of our youth as I could reach to come over quickly and get it straight from the horse's mouth! I instructed them to just listen, not argue, and come back again the next week after they had boned up on the Mormon faith. Listen again the second Sunday and after that respond. The Mormon evangelists were delighted to have 15 youth listen to their spiel and were willing to come again the next Sunday! After their second lecture on the following Sunday, our kids asked them questions. "Do you know for sure you're going to heaven?" They didn't and our kids started giving personal testimonies until the Mormon speaker got wistful and wished HE had such assurance. Their leader rushed him out of the room and they never came back.

Besides all the requested workshops that were scheduled for most school holidays, I had offered the kids, "If you really mean business with God and want to grow in your relationship with Him, I'll commit to helping you <u>individually </u>every week. There will be assignments. If you are too busy to do them, I'll be too busy to help you. It's up to you." No one could say I was being partial to some. They began coming at their school noon hour if nearby, or after school or I'd meet them someplace. Very simply they'd recite the Scripture verses they were memorizing, nuggets from their Quiet-Time that week, and tell of their struggles and victories of that week. I discipled them individually in this way.

My Sunday School class grew to around 25 regulars. We used a variety of formats, like dividing into buzz groups of 3 or 4 to dig into a passage, apply it and then share their discoveries with the group at large. When my furlough time came and I couldn't find a suitable person to take my class, two of my high school fellows came to me saying, "Don't know if this sounds too presumptuous, but we wonder if you'd dare to entrust this class to us in your year's absence!!" I was thrilled. One of those two fellows is a Free Church pastor today!

We began planning together a very intentional cycle of weekly youth meetings. We'd start with an outing or social with a purpose. It was not just for themselves but to invite as many non-Christian friends as possible. We'd get acquainted, play hard, sing lustily and then simmer down to a worship and testimony time. One in our group would give personal testimony like this: "We've all had a good time here today. You can find a good time in other places too; but we have something here that you won't easily find other places. We'll ask _____ to tell you about it." A personal testimony from one in our group would follow as to how Christ had given meaning and purpose to his or her life. "If you want this for your life also, come back next Saturday evening to a meeting planned especially for you to learn how you can enjoy this new life and fellowship with God, too." An evangelistic meeting would follow and then meetings to strengthen the new believers in their faith.

SCHOOL OUTREACH

Our Living Springs youth began reaching out to their school classmates. I remember one evangelistic meeting where they had brought around 20 non-Christian classmates. At the close they didn't dismiss them; rather the Christian kids pulled up their chairs, one Christian kid with one non-Christian, two by two, with open Bibles and showed them how to find Jesus! What a beautiful sight.

Our kids were not without their own emotional and personal problems that were often home related. Simon, for example, had been given away as a child to a relative aunt to raise. He had little emotional security. At one incident on an outing he blurted out bitterly to me, "You don't <u>really</u> care about me." Actually, I have found that I grow to really love the people for whom I pray. I had prayed so much for Simon and had come to so deeply care for him and every aspect of his life that I was speechless at his bitter comment. I just burst into tears. Without any wise counseling from me and without even a word, Simon knew then that he was deeply loved. He even mentioned this incident 45 years later at our wedding reception about the impact of those tears!

Eventually, Simon came to the States, earned his PhD and taught science in a Chicago University. More amazing is that Simon was eventually elected to be on the executive board of the Evangelical Free Church of America! He commented to me, "The Free Church of America sent you to Hong Kong where you touched my life. Now I'm part of the Executive Board of the Free Church of America sending missionaries all over the world. Missions have now come full circle!" God's awesome ways! His incredible working in one unlikely life! I wear a dress that was a surprise gift. It was made for me by Simon's sister and mailed to me from Hong Kong!

Here's another example of God's working where I was without words. A high school senior, Stephen, who was rather new to our youth group, was crushed by his father's illness and death. It was just before Stephen's school certification exams so he couldn't study to pass those exams. Without a good score on those exams, four years of high school wouldn't count. It seemed to him as if his whole future was blown. He would now be the bread winner for his family with little hope of a good job. He came to me with this crushing news and we prayed together. I visited his mother in her grief who began coming to our women's meetings and eventually trusted Christ as did some of Stephen's siblings. I took him to be a Christian already. After some weeks, Stephen dropped out of church and youth meetings for quite a while. I was worried for him. When I ran into him unexpectedly at a funeral, I expressed my concern for his absence. He replied proudly that now he had a great job at one of Hong Kong's ritzy hotels as bell-boy and was making good money. Now he didn't need church or God anymore! Again I had no wise words to counsel him. I just burst into tears beyond my control. He testified years later in our seminary how those tears brought him under conviction. "Why would that Western lady care so much about my dropping out of church?" He came back, was truly saved and became my student in seminary. Today at this writing, Stephen pastors a Free Church in one of Hong Kong's high-rise buildings. Certainly not because of any wise words from me!

Giving individual help to disciple so many of these youth meant my time was squeezed. I saw the need was great and the laborers too few; so I began to pray the Lord of the harvest to raise up full time workers from our Living Springs youth group. I asked the Lord, "How many should I pray for?" I settled on asking for a dozen full time workers, eventually, for His harvest from our small youth group! Was I asking too much? I prayed often for this incredible request. Would that prayer ever be answered?

John, our youth chairman, who was saved at that youth conference, had often expressed his life dream to go to sea and to become a ship captain. As king of his ship, he could sail the world wherever he pleased. Now after God had transformed him in his youth, he sensed God's call on his life for full time service. How could he train for the ministry? His mother was hotly antagonistic to the Gospel. He was so afraid of her. Her son, a minister? Perish the thought! John shared this fear with our youth group. "I sense God's call on my life. I should give my life to serve Him with the strength of my youth; but I am too afraid of my Mom. When you give a bouquet of flowers to someone you love, you don't wait until the flowers are wilted. You give them while they're fresh. I should give my life, my bouquet, to God while I'm young with the strength of my youth." But John's bouquet wilted. He went to sea for his life work. John eventually became the first Chinese licensed sea captain. A great national honor! He sailed the world but he couldn't shake off the hand of God on his life. He finally took early retirement, went through Regent Seminary in Vancouver and at this writing is now pastoring a Chinese church in Canada.

Several others, too, from that group went on to seminary and full-time ministry. I can't tell you all their stories. Some of them served faithfully in significant secular positions, as salt and light where God put them, in raising their Christian families and serving faithfully in their local church.

Samuel, for example, went into the restaurant business in Sydney, Australia. He used his restaurant on Sunday mornings for the start of a Chinese Free Church. That church eventually grew into four large Chinese Free churches in Sydney alone.

Today, after several decades, my early prayer for God to call a dozen from that youth group into full time service has been answered. A few of them did go directly into the ministry. Years later, one after another of that youth group have left good jobs, taken early retirement plus training and have since been serving the Lord full time for longer or shorter periods. I can now count a full dozen of them who for longer or shorter periods have served in Hong Kong, China, Canada, Europe and the United States. God's timing and God's ways are so much higher than mine!

EPILOGUE ON PETER

Peter and his family moved to Vancouver, British Columbia, Canada, where he married Ying, a sweet committed Christian girl also from our Living Springs EFC youth group. They bought a big house where they cared for Peter's aging parents. His father was very deaf

as well as dead set against the gospel; but Peter led his
dad to salvation on his death bed. Peter's mother trusted
Christ much sooner and lived to be 100. Although she
developed Alzheimer's so that she was difficult to care
for, Peter and his family lovingly and tenderly cared for
her at home like she was a special treasure, a delicate
fragile doll. Strangely, every morning when she would
read the Scriptures, her mind was clear!

After my retirement I routed my trips to and from
Hong Kong via Vancouver to stay with Peter and Ying
en route. On one visit, shy little Ying told me that she
had started a Bible study for the Chinese mothers in the
neighborhood which involved around a dozen ladies.
She especially mentioned one lady, Monica, who was
not a Christian. "I wish you could talk with her." Peter
suggested, "Let's have her and her husband, Allan, over
for a visit after supper so you can talk with them about
the Lord."

They came, but Allan who was brilliant and well-
read in philosophy, talked circles around me. Rather
than try to reason with him, I asked him, "Allan, if you
knew this God were true, would you follow him?" He
answered "Sure." I told him how to search for the truth.
"Start reading from the Gospel of John every day.
Before you read, pray to God telling Him that you are
searching for Him. If you find him to be true, you will
follow Him; then read the Scriptures, underlining verses
that especially speak to you. When you finish reading
for the day, pray back to God your impressions." I

asked him if he would be willing to do that. He said "Yes," but he didn't do it. However, Monica did begin to search for God that way.

One day, something unusual happened. A Chinese lady, a total stranger, came to her door and offered to lend Monica a video. She said she would return later for it. It happened to be the Jesus video in Cantonese, Monica's language. Monica watched the video and believed on Jesus. They never found out who that lady was who brought the video and she never returned for it. Was she an angel?

Now Allan was extremely angry with Monica because Jesus was now first in her life and not him! He forbade her to read the Bible or go to church and he threatened to divorce her and return to Hong Kong for another wife! Monica was so broken hearted. She hyper-ventilated and passed out so Allan called the paramedics to revive her. He was afraid to lose her so he took back his harsh words and promised that she could read the Bible and go to church. He would even go with her! He did not go with her but now she was released to grow as a believer.

Another time when I was passing through Vancouver and staying with Ying and Peter, Monica called. She was upset because the Jehovah's Witnesses had been coming to her place and confusing her with their doctrine. She said, "I wish Hui Kwoo Neung (my Chinese name) were here to help me." Ying said, "She's here. She just came last night."

Monica came over and shared other problems, too. Her aged mother from a country village in China had come to live with them and their four year old son would react so violently whenever Jesus was mentioned. Their pastor, a former Free Church missionary, suggested the four year old might be demon possessed!

I suggested that we go together to Monica's house. There her four year old was quietly playing on the computer. I met the old grandma, whom I feared may have at one time, when the child was sick, dedicated him to some idol or spirit in exchange for his health. (This is not uncommon among the village people.) I said to Monica, "We must go to every room in your house claiming Jesus' victory on the cross and rebuking any evil spirits that might be lurking there. This we did. Finally we laid hands on the child and claimed Jesus' victory and protection over him. I was told later that when the name of Jesus was mentioned, he never had those fits again!

Lastly, we prayed for the old grandmother who spoke a village dialect. Through Monica's interpretation, I explained the Gospel to the old woman and she immediately responded positively to believe on Jesus! I doubted that she really understood because she was deeply steeped in idol worship and had the untrained mind of a village woman without schooling; but I was wrong. She firmly believed and became an active witness for Jesus!

Now Allan was a computer whiz so I called his office to explain that I was going to Hong Kong and wanted to do email there but I didn't know how to connect up with AOL there. Could he help me? "Sure, come to my office with your laptop." Still on the phone, he added, "Say, this Jesus that you've been talking about stands head and shoulders above all the other philosophers!" Later in his office we talked computer for a bit and then I asked him what he meant by that statement. He said that in John 8 where the woman taken in adultery was to be stoned, Jesus said, *"Let him who is without sin cast the first stone."* Allan said that in all the philosophers he had read there was nothing to compare with that. I asked him, "Allan, are you ready to believe on Jesus?" The tears came streaming down his face and he said, "Yes." That day, Allan too, was born into God's family and together Allan and Monica grew to become leaders in Peter's church.

In fact, Peter, a layman, was instrumental in starting the first Chinese Evangelical Free Church in Canada. That start was in Burnaby, British Columbia. It grew to start another Chinese Free church in New Richmond, another in Vancouver, four in Calgary and now they are spread across Canada to reach its heavy Chinese population. Peter's son, Philip, is today at this writing the youth pastor of the Vancouver Chinese Evangelical Free Church.

All this originally came from such a small, unlikely youth group that held so little promise. I've observed that God's work really begins with a prayer burden as God shares His heart with <u>us.</u>

STUDENT MOVEMENT AT
HONG KONG UNIVERSITY

When I returned to Hong Kong again after two years of recuperating from undulant fever, I felt heavily burdened for Hong Kong's high school students. My focus then was on the youth of the Living Springs Evangelical Free Church. After many months, God sent revival to that group. I wished for some Christian organization like "Youth for Christ" or "Young Life" to unite the Christian students to have the courage to be active witnesses in their high schools. This needed to be an interdenominational work. If I tried to start something, some churches might think I was trying to steal their sheep! Furthermore, I had no such experience.

About that time in 1955-56, God sent Gwen Wong, an American born Chinese gal, to Hong Kong on a mission to Hong Kong's English university. Gwen lived with me so I got a blow-by-blow account of what God was doing there through her. David Adeney, who was general secretary of the Far East International Fellowship of Evangelical Students (IFES), had sent her ahead to lay the ground work for his coming later to minister among the Hong Kong University students. Rev. Adeney had been greatly used of God in universities of China shortly before the Communist takeover to fuel a powerful spiritual revival and student movement back then. Hong Kong boasted just one English-language university, which accepted only the top students from local English speaking high schools. The University was a highly respected, prestigious school and was difficult to gain entrance.

Gwen's task was to seek to turn the university's "Christian Association" into a vital Christian function and witness. For years it had functioned as an official extra-curricular activity of the university but it only met around Christmas time to become a choir, singing Christmas carols, secular Christmas songs as well as tavern songs. The real Christian students wanted no part of it. Gwen's task was to first get the real Christian students revitalized by getting into the Word, and eventually into that Christian Association to make it a vital Christian influence on campus.

Gwen's strategy was first to gain a foothold in the university's dorms with her ukulele and her personality to organize the true Christian students into small Bible studies that they could lead themselves, asking such simple questions on Bible passages, as "What example is there to follow", "What command to obey", "What sin to avoid", "What promise to claim", "What does this passage teach me about God and His will for my life?" Many such dorm Bible studies blossomed, strengthening and unifying the Christian students. They even attracted the non-Christians. Gwen persuaded the Christian students to get into that official Christian Association, become a part of that choir, and revitalize that official "Christian Association". This they did; but they upset the University chancellor (who directed the choir) by refusing to sing some of the songs that did not honor the Lord. As a result, the chancellor left. A keen Christian, highly respected professor at the University, Dr. King, came to help the Christian Association.

David Adeney also arrived with his university student work experience. They turned this limited, seasonal Christmas choir into powerful weekly Gospel rallies and summer conferences that impacted the whole campus. The only possible explanation for all that happened thereafter is that the Holy Spirit of God moved to bring a revival that swept that campus. Their weekly rallies and summer conferences began drawing one tenth of the student body to their meetings. Many lives were transformed. The Christian Association became the largest, most dynamic extra-curricular activity on campus with unsaved students coming to Christ week after week. These life changes included students that I had known personally and had sought to lead to Christ since their high school days. I was thrilled to attend some of their rallies and see God at work. The whole university campus was impacted and the effects of this revival began to be felt throughout the colony.

STUDENT MOVEMENT IN
THE HIGH SCHOOLS

Actually, God was working on many fronts among Hong Kong students in those days. I was blessed to have Gwen living with me as she began infiltrating the University dorms. I was excited to hear what God was doing at the University. I begged Gwen to start something for the high school students; but her total focus was on the University. While I had been discipling a high school teacher from our church, who in turn was mentoring a high school girl from her youth group, news leaked out that her girl was quietly meeting daily with two other classmates in their school to pray for their unsaved classmates! This was exciting news to me. It looked like God was up to something!

AN UPSIDE DOWN PYRAMID

When Gwen heard this news she said, "When men build something, they start with a huge effort like a pyramid which eventually peters out to nothing. When God starts something, it's like a pyramid upside down. It usually begins with a prayer burden and then grows into something big." I contacted a Christian teacher I knew in that high school, Mary Holland, inviting her to come for supper. Gwen and I told her of the three Free Church girls in her school who were burdened and praying for their classmates. Mary could hardly believe it. She had come from England to teach in this all-girls' "mission school" and hoped to have some spiritual impact. She'd started a small Bible study with a few girls. Sadly, at exam time, it dwindled down to zero. She felt ready to return to England. Upon our urging her to re-start that Bible Study, she replied, "O.K. Gwen, if you'll speak the first week". She doubted that any girls would come. Surprise! Thirty girls showed up! From six dwindling down to zero, and now suddenly thirty girls? How come? Because God was moving three girls to pray daily for their classmates!

Two weeks later the girls met again. Now it was my turn to lead them. Not only had their numbers grown, but several girls requested permission to stand up and say something. "You all know me and what I've been like. Within the last two weeks I have trusted Christ personally and He has turned my life around. This is what Christ has done for me...…" Their simple, open sharing drew tears and goose bumps! You can imagine the effect on those girls. I found it easy to speak after that! In the following few weeks about fifteen of those girls also trusted Christ.

If God was moving so in this high school, what about other high schools where we had contacts? God brought together Christian students in more high schools for daily prayer and weekly Bible studies. This thing spread. As the newly revived university students caught a vision for the high schools, they, with Gwen and David Adeney, helped them to plan, organize and lead bi-monthly evangelistic rallies for them. The high school students would enthusiastically bring their unsaved classmates and vie to be the largest block in the meeting wearing their school's uniform. They were excited to see so many of their classmates trust Christ.

Hong Kong had a number of "mission high schools" affiliated with local churches. Many of these churches and schools were doctrinally liberal and their churches were threatened by the evangelical fervor of these Christian youth. These youth were their own young people who were teaching in their own Sunday Schools and spreading this evangelical teaching within their church!

Seniors in one mission school were so hungry for the Word of God that they were meeting off campus during their lunch hour to study the Word together. When their church and school leadership heard of this, the students were forbidden to meet any more for those Bible studies or even to hold those evangelical false beliefs! Unless they complied, they would be kicked out of school. Seven of them were in their final year of high school with stiff matriculation exams coming up. To fail those exams would mean no high school credit. It was a hard test but the students chose to stand their ground for faith and conscience in spite of the risk. Yes, they were kicked out of school at such a critical time. The news of the stand taken by those mission high school seniors reached and challenged many other schools, inspiring and invigorating many other students in their commitment to Christ. Praise God, each of the seven students, who had been kicked out, passed their colony-wide matriculation exams with flying colors! They entered Hong Kong University to join and energize the revival fires already burning there.

There was excitement at those rallies as so many of their friends trusted Christ. This movement of high

school students putting their heads together each
morning for united prayer and weekly Bible studies
spread to other high schools until about 40 of the
top English language high schools of the colony were
participating. This was true of government, Catholic
and Protestant high schools with the students meeting
either on or off campus as the situation dictated.
These enthusiastic kids eventually fed into the
University, swelling the salvation decisions at the joint
evangelistic rallies and extending those revival fires.
The Christian Association was blessed by the lives and
messages of David Adeney, Dr. King and some spirit-
filled national pastors. I was blessed beyond measure
just to watch from the sidelines and see God at work in
so many lives.

Through the years I have kept loosely in touch by
phone or email with some of the active leaders in that
student movement although now they are all in their
seventies! Many of them have maintained contact with
each other to share God's activity in their lives. Prior to
writing this account, I double-checked with several of
them for accuracy and heard that even after 10 years,
the student-led Bible studies still continued in many
high schools.

Strong leaders emerged from the university
student movement to be used by God to form
organizations such as the Christian Nurses Fellowship
which impacted hundreds of Hong Kong nurses, a
Fellowship of Christian teachers, and a Graduate
Christian Fellowship which sponsored a Christian

reading room and book store with full time, live-in Chinese staff (like Mildred Young) to council, guide and minister to the students. The whole movement mushroomed beyond our farthest dreams. Later God sent Ada Lum, a very effective Inter-Varsity trainer, to Hong Kong to follow up this movement and establish these new leaders in the Word.

At the thirty- year anniversary of the beginning of this student movement, many graduates, whose lives had been so impacted by that revival, returned from around the world to celebrate. They filled the largest Holiday Inn ballroom in Hong Kong to reunite and share their memories and how God had used this movement in their lives ever since.

To this day a large percent of the Christians in Hong Kong will tell you how they found Christ in their high school or university days through this student movement. Indeed, we witnessed a pyramid upside down that began with a prayer burden.

 **Chapter 6**

GOD'S AMAZING LEADING

SEMINARY STORY

In the 1960s I began teaching English and Inductive Bible study part-time at our Evangel Seminary in Hong Kong. I used my furloughs in the late 1960s and early 1970s to finish my M. Div. degree at Trinity Divinity School, Deerfield, Illinois, and continued teaching at our Evangel Seminary, mostly fulltime for the next 35 years.

Seminary teaching blessed me in two ways: first, the blessing of saturation in the Word as I taught it and, second, my close involvement with the students and their personal lives. Classes were small when I began teaching there, less than a dozen in a class. I was able to visit some of their parents, too, and had the joy of leading some of them to trust in Christ. Later the classes grew up to a hundred per class in the evening courses for laymen. My favorite courses to teach were Old Testament, Inductive Bible study and Personal Evangelism.

Not all students were equally gifted. I urged several of them who did exceptional work to go on after graduation from Evangel Seminary to further schooling and to return as teachers in our seminary. They did and God even led one, Maureen Yeung, to return first as a teacher and eventually as Seminary president for eight years!

It was also very gratifying to see some freshmen come with a heart for God, but showing little evidence of needed gifts and then, after three years, to see God's hand on their lives, gifting and transforming them into keenly effective workmen for God!

In the early 1970s, our seminary faced two crises where we saw God's marvelous undertaking. First the seminary was severely unfunded for its growing operation. The United States Free Churches assumed that our local Hong Kong Free churches could support the entire seminary while our seven struggling local Hong Kong churches expected our United States churches to carry the load. There was a communication breakdown. Our president, Dr. John Pao, felt he could not run a quality seminary on a shoestring so, in discouragement, he eventually resigned, to take effect two years later. This was before the days of computers or copy machines for communication with supporters. All we had was a Gestetner mimeograph machine.

This was a growing experience for us all. God burdened me to spend a whole summer gathering addresses of United States Free Churches, Women's Missionary Societies, my own supporters and anyone I knew with a heart for missions. My goal was to flood them with information about Evangel Seminary, about what God was doing there and to share the vision of its potential for the Kingdom. I shared my deep heart burden for trained workers to reach the six million mainly refugees then packed into Hong Kong as well as our opportunities for reaching out to China.

I latched on to God's promise to Abraham for descendants as many as the stars of the sky and sand of the sea shore. "God, give us spiritual descendants like that, a chain reaction through the lives and ministry of these students to produce disciples beyond number." We needed more than money. We needed God's people who shared His heart and vision for this ministry to partner with us in persistent prayer. Many did. With their prayers came funding as well. We became partners together in spiritual warfare. Long before that proposed president's resignation deadline, God had answered prayer. Our prayer team swelled, the financial picture changed and Dr. Pao withdrew his resignation!

Also in the 1970s, Evangel Seminary's faculty and students faced another crisis and a remarkable answer to prayer. Our facilities were deteriorating, leaking and needing both renovation and expansion. Although operating expenses were by then being met, the cost of the needed renovation was far beyond reach. The cost was too much to even ask of our supporters whether local or State side.

God is glorified by the praises of His people. In 2 Chronicles 20:20-22 where Israel faced a desperate military crisis, King Jehosophat sent the choir ahead of his army. "*When the choir began to sing and to praise, God sent ambushment against the enemy.* " With this in mind, I typed a Gestetner stencil to challenge our partners back home to do the same, to participate in such a miracle, by praising God in advance for providing for this renovation in such a way that all could see that only He could do it and then watch with us for a huge miracle. I mailed that stencil to the friend who did our mailings back home to save on overseas postage, and then I dropped that stencil in an envelope into a local Hong Kong mailbox. "Now Lord, we're all waiting to see what You will do!" God's reputation was on the line.

We didn't have long to wait. Later <u>THAT SAME AFTERNOON</u> Dr. Pao got a phone call from a wealthy Hong Kong Christian business man (not of our denomination) who expressed how impressed he was with what he had observed of some graduates of our school. God had laid our seminary on his heart. "If you need to enlarge or remodel your seminary, send me the bill and I will pick up the tab! " Major renovations were thereby completed at the seminary that year of 1973 as we praised God together in advance.

ADVENTURE WITH GOD

"Immeasurably more than we could ask or imagine!" is a quote that describes my experience of God's miraculous guidance that fall day. It was an adventure with God that caused even a non-Christian Communist official to conclude: "It must be that God helped you!"

It all started on a Hong Kong public holiday that preceded our seminary's Anniversary Homecoming Day. Our seminary, Evangel Theological College (ES for short), had two week-days of holiday in a row that was significant to this story.

Another coincidence was that although a visa application for China takes several days to process, I already had an unused visa for China! Since my previously intended trip had been postponed, my way was now clear to enter China anytime. I was physically available and my heart wide open to God's leading, however strange.

EMERGENCY CALL

At eight a.m. on that holiday Monday morning, I got an emergency phone call from Chicago. This was the message: A Free Church lady from the Chicago area, while teaching English in China, was impressed by the potential and fine spirit of a Chinese scholar teaching University-level English there. She dreamed of bringing him to the United States for a year's study at Trinity College where he could advance his English and find Jesus. She named him "Samuel."

Her church backed this idea, sponsored him, bought his plane ticket and Trinity College accepted him as a student. Besides attending college, he could teach a course on Chinese culture at a Chicago school for exceptional children. Because he had ties of a wife and child back home, the Chinese government granted permission for him to go; but when his Korean Airlines plane arrived at Chicago's O'Hare airport without him, there was no way to contact him to discover why he was not on it. A week passed without word and Trinity College had started.

FRUSTRATING HOLDUP

In the meantime Samuel was delayed up country by China's bureaucratic red tape until AFTER his plane had left Hong Kong! Was his chance of a lifetime slipping away? He prayed to that God in heaven that he had heard about from the American teacher. Finally, a week later he reached Sam Jan, the city bordering Hong Kong. There he faced another problem.

Without his Korean Air Lines ticket in hand, the Hong Kong authorities would not let him enter the colony! That plane ticket he so desperately needed was beyond his reach. It was waiting for him at Hong Kong's International Airport! He couldn't get there! Again he prayed.

Help came through a kindly customs officer who took pity on him. He helped him to send a fax letter to Chicago and to make an overseas phone call to his American friends to explain his dilemma and to leave his contact information.

COMPLICATIONS

The phone message to me from Chicago that morning requested that I pick up his plane ticket in the Hong Kong airport and deliver it to him across the border of China. It sounded simple enough but there were complications due to an expired ticket and it being a public holiday which meant that all airline offices were closed.

In my Living Springs Sunday School class of about 25 high school, college and career youth was a young fellow who worked for Singapore Airlines. Since it was a holiday, I phoned him at his home for advice. He said to forget the Korean Airlines ticket. I should meet him across the harbor at his office and he would write me a fake ticket for Singapore Airlines, just to get Samuel into Hong Kong.

By mid-afternoon, with the fake ticket in hand, I was on my way for an hour's train-ride across Hong Kong to the Sam Jan/ Hong Kong border. There, through the endless rig-a-ma-role of checks by immigration officials, health officers, customs inspection, etc., I was finally cleared to cross into China. Now the task of finding Samuel would come!

The city of Sam Jan was unfamiliar to me and everyone was speaking Mandarin instead of Cantonese! The address that he had left over the phone to his American friends was of course in ENGLISH: "Sam Jan Guest Hostel." What would that be in Chinese so I could direct the taxi? No one recognized that English name. The Chinese have a wide array of possible terms for hotel, ranging from the humblest inn, dormitory or motel to most swanky hotel.

Another problem: the street address was a main artery with dozens of lanes branching off like the legs of a centipede and all using the same trunk-street's name! If that wasn't problem enough, I had neither street number nor Chinese name for the hostel.

I must first find an English speaker who could translate "Guest Hostel" into Chinese for me. Maybe someone at a high class hotel could help me. After picking a term at random for "hotel," I told the taxi driver to take me to a classy one. I was really looking for an interpreter.

ADVENTURE

Humanly speaking, finding Samuel under such circumstances was worse than hopeless. Yet God had already overcome so many obstacles for me by preparing my visa in advance, arranging the only date that month I was available to go, and supplying a fake plane ticket on a public holiday. Surely He could direct me all the way. I settled back in my taxi seat, amused now to watch how God would solve this one; <u>HIS</u> problem, not mine! "Another adventure with You, Lord! Let's see what you'll do THIS time!"

FAT CHANCE!

The taxi dropped me at a fairly upscale hotel that was beyond both Samuel's means and mine. I asked the lady at the information desk to give me the name of the fanciest hotel in town where someone might know English. She brightened, dialed a number and handed me the phone. "Here, it's my husband, and he knows English." I asked him, "Please, could you give me a likely term for 'guest hostel' in Chinese so I can find a certain hostel?" His response was, "Why don't you stay at that hotel where my wife works?" I explained that I was looking for a certain scholar who was trying to get to America and I told him briefly of Samuel's dilemma. His irrelevant response was "What city in the United States is he going to?" I thought impatiently under my breath, "What does his city destination have to do with the price of peanuts in January!!!!" However, I restrained myself and replied politely, "Chicago."

Next question, "Is his ticket for Korean Airlines?" (I nearly dropped the phone.) He turned out to be the VERY SAME CUSTOMS OFFICER who had helped Samuel to send a fax letter and international phone call! Now, figure the ratio of 'chance' on THAT one! Out of a city of then 400,000 people, my random efforts would lead me to the exact customs officer who had helped Samuel at the border!

GOD'S HUMOR

The customs officer said on the phone that he did not know where the fellow was staying, but he would recognize him on sight and he was willing to come to help me find him! This officer was a real gentleman. He carried my heavy suitcase the whole way, on and off buses, up and down bridges and across busy intersections. Little did he know that aside from my toothbrush and PJ's inside, the contents were all Bibles! Thankfully he never asked why I had such a heavy bag for just one overnight! The wry humor of God to arrange a customs officer to carry my Bibles!!

That evening, after endless walking, bus rides, climbing stairs to bridges over intersections, milling with traffic, asking directions and general searching, we finally found the Sam Jan Guest Hostel and Samuel, who recognized the officer immediately. On seeing the plane ticket in my hand, he was beside himself with joy. He began dancing in circles around the lobby, with chop sticks in one hand and an enamel rice bowl in the other, and telling the gathering crowd over and over how he had prayed to this fantastic God who had so remarkably answered his prayer. The commotion brought more crowds in from the busy street who all heard his testimony.

When the customs officer realized how hopelessly remote had been any CHANCE of my finding him, he exclaimed incredulously, "It must be that God helped you!" I asked, "Are you a Christian then?" He was not. He refused any tip for his trouble but he accepted a simple rice meal with Samuel and his dormitory buddy and me. I stayed alone in the women's dormitory of the hostel that night. Samuel and his buddy first worked with gusto using many buckets of hot water and a stiff broom to clean up the women's shower and toilet for me. I slept that hot night on a straw mat over bed-boards which were enclosed by a mosquito net. Early the next morning I sneaked off alone to deposit my satchel of Bibles at a prearranged place before I had a tea house breakfast with Samuel and his buddy.

At breakfast Samuel exclaimed over and over his awe of this God. His buddy said, "Years ago, an old man told me about God but I didn't believe it. Now I can't help but believe." I shared the Gospel with Samuel and his buddy. There in the crowded and noisy public restaurant, they both bowed their heads and humbly invited Jesus into their lives.

It took me most of the day in Hong Kong to resolve his ticket issues. In the market I bought him new jeans and a couple of T-shirts. (His shirts looked like they'd been washed in the Yellow River!)

That night, still awe-struck by the flood of overwhelming events of the past two days, my heart was overflowing with thanksgiving and joy. I celebrated our seminary's Homecoming feast with Samuel, my guest from China who was now sharply dressed and a brother in Christ. The next day Samuel was on his flight to Chicago and Trinity College.

The following week back at our Living Springs Peace Study Center, I shared Samuel's story. There, two more young college fellows were searching for concrete evidence that this God is true. Upon hearing Samuel's story, they finally believed and trusted Christ as Savior and Lord. They, too, were added to God's family. Such is a ripple effect when we are available to God! Walking with God and being led by His Spirit is an endless adventure!

Knute Hjalmar Ekblad

Missionary Ekblad

Wedded to Alma - 1918

Wedded to Selma - 1925

Wedded to Bertha - 1937

Wedded to Florence 1960

Missionary Prayer Card

Paul and Doris

1929 Chevrolet Touring Car

Mongolian Yurt

Mr. and Mrs. Gunzel with the Ekblad family

Martyr's Cemetery

Ekblad family in Trade River – Bertha, Hjalmar, Doris, Paul

Great wall with Camels

Mongol Congregation at Pailingmiao 1934

Gunzel's first Mongolian Church

Caravan at Mission station 1937

Loading Camels

Mongolia of my childhood

Bereft of Mother in China, Children Will Live Here

Doris and Paul Ekblad, Who Left St. Paul With Parents in 1934 for Far East Mission Station, Sent Back to Make Home With Aunt.

Two motherless Minnesota children were nearing today the end of a 7,000-mile journey they have made alone from China to St. Paul.

Seven-year-old Doris Ekblad and her brother, Paul, 6, will get here at 7:45 A. M. Thursday to live with an aunt, Mrs. John Swanson, 747 East Jessamine street.

The youngsters arrived Monday in San Francisco from Shanghai, which they left June 30 on the steamship General Lee. They traveled under watchful eyes of ship and railroad officials.

Children of Rev. Hjalmer Ekblad, a Minnesota missionary in Kweisui, Suiyuan province, China, the youngsters lost their mother in March. She died in Kweisui, a town near the Mongolian border, after a long illness. The father decided he could not care adequately for Doris and Paul, and Mrs. Swanson offered to mother them.

"I'll have to start raising a family again," said Mrs. Swanson. "My own family, a daughter and two boys, are grown up now. But, I'm glad to have Doris and Paul."

Both the Ekblad children were born in Minnesota. They left St. Paul in August, 1934, for China. Rev. Mr. Ekblad previously had been a missionary there.

MOTHERLESS PAIR RETURN

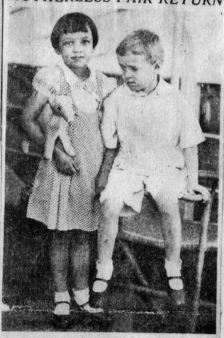

DORIS AND PAUL EKBLAD.

Doris and Paul Ekblad return to U.S. 1936

Doris as a small child

Doris college days

Doris at 23

Doris at Evangel Seminary

Graveside service for Selma

Chapter 7

TRAVEL MERCIES

RETURN TO MONGOLIA

In 1972 President Nixon had gone to China and policies there began to change. China became more open to the outside world. They began to allow overseas Chinese to return for visits. It had been very tightly closed before. By 1982, I began toying with the idea of going back to my childhood home in Inner Mongolia. Dad had passed away ten years before without ever hearing from his friends back there. Had the church survived the persecution? Was there still a church existing back there in Inner Mongolia? Had his lifework and sacrifice paid off? I wanted to find out.

Because I was only six when I left, I would not know how to find my old home there; but Asta Nelsen was a Swedish Baptist missionary in Hong Kong who began her service in Inner Mongolia. In fact she lived for a time on our mission station. Since she was there as an adult, she would be most able to find our old home. I contacted her about this idea.

"Vell, Vee can pray about dat," she said. When I applied in Hong Kong for a visa to the capital city of

Inner Mongolia, I was told, "We can only grant visas to the two major coastal cities, Shanghai and Beijing. It is impossible for you to go farther inland. You can go to Beijing and try to apply there." Asta wrote to two old missionary friends, Olia Simeonson and her son Roland, who were both born in Mongolia. They had been working many years in Japan since Mongolia was closed.

When Olia, 72 years old, heard that Asta and I planned a trip back up there, she begged, "Oh, could Roland and I go with you? My husband and I had hoped to do so someday but now he is with the Lord." Asta said, "She has a bad heart and if she goes up there and sees her old friends and gets excited, who knows vat vee veel have on our hands!" It was a good thing they came because it was Olia's white hair and the Chinese respect for age that got us into places that no Westerners had been for over 30 years.

Asta's Christian friends in Beijing showed us the city while we waited for our visas inland. I had brought along pictures of my childhood in Mongolia and they got passed all around the visa office. The Chinese have a great sense of history and these interested them greatly. I feared that I wouldn't get them all back. They said to return in three days and they would have an answer for us.

After three days the visas were GRANTED! So we took the 7:30 train that evening for Inner Mongolia. I woke up at 4:00 a.m. and it was already light outside. This was mid-June. I saw communes built along the tracks and electric wires. The land that the Mongols had feared to till, lest they would let out evil spirits, had been planted and cultivated. I saw real progress in Mongolia.

When we arrived at our city, we were taken to stay at a large hotel that the missionaries recognized as the former Catholic convent. There were wide tree-lined streets and two story buildings! Nothing like what we remembered. Asta said, "We have no addresses and we don't want to be known as missionaries. I have little hope that we can find the church!" But that's what I had come for!!

GRASSLANDS TOUR

We were offered a tour up over the mountains to the Mongolian grasslands. It was the tourist thing to do and we didn't want to be recognized as missionaries. There were Chinese tourists in our van as well. We stopped at a Friday fair where all the locals bring their handcrafts and goods to sell. With such a crowd my dad would surely have preached to them but we could say nothing. This was Communist territory.

The places that we visited brought back many childhood memories. Piles of camel dung to be used for winter fuel were as high as the yurt (a tent made of camel hair felt) beside them. We saw a wheelbarrow lined with pieces of broken mirror to reflect the sun with which they could boil a kettle of water on a rack above the mirror in forty minutes. Each yurt had a wind generator to produce electricity for their TV! Outside the city on our return trip of this packaged tour, we stopped at a high pagoda and climbed to the top to overlook the city.

INSIDE THE OLD CITY

We discovered that we had been in the New City. The Old City was right beside it. It was much the same as when we left it over forty years before. We tried to pick out the roofs of the three churches that we had known there. We asked the driver if he could drive us into the old city. He said the roads are too narrow; but he'd take us to the edge and give us 20 minutes inside. We walked fast. It was just as I had remembered it. Asta stopped to ask an old gentleman who was squatting along the street and reading the paper, "Old Man, do you know if there is a Christian church in this city?" "Yes", he answered, "and they're having a service right now." A younger man led us there. The courtyard was filled with bicycles and the dwelling inside was full of people. This was 5:00 o'clock on Saturday afternoon.

A Chinese man came to the door and called out in English, "Are you Christians?" We said, "Yes." "Oh, come in, come in." We were the first outside guests that they'd had in some 30 years and we couldn't stay. I offered to go and deal with the tour car while Asta, Olia and Roland stayed for the service. The next morning (Sunday) we were back there for the service. I had thought to bring the pictures of Dad and our childhood there, but I brought the wrong manila envelope by mistake! I asked to borrow a bicycle and biked all the way back to our hotel for the pictures. The service was underway when I got back. They had saved a seat for me. I did not understand the message but they sure sang from their hearts. When the service ended, folks turned to ask who we were. I had Xeroxed the inside page of Dad's Bible which I showed them of his signatures and also some pictures. Their first words were, "And how is your brother Paul?" I realized I was talking to the same people that I had said good-by to 46 years before! I will never forget the love they poured out that afternoon. They said "This is just a small meeting place that the government has given us but we have over a thousand Christians belonging to this church. We rotate coming to services seven days a week. To meet all who knew you as a child, you must come a full seven days!"

BAPTISMAL SERVICE

That afternoon there was a baptismal service. Since the government has put all the churches together, one baptismal service will be by sprinkling and the next by immersion. This Sunday 43 people were sprinkled. The pastor called them up four or five at a time. He gave each one a very personal dedicatory prayer and sprinkled with water. As the afternoon wore on, I wondered if these old pastors could stand that long. One of the ladies being baptized was a Mongol. She said, "I understand spoken Chinese but I can't read it. Is there such a thing as a Mongolian Bible?" I said that I would try to find out.

Asta and Olia knew the three pastors of this church. They all knew my dad. The pastors lived in quarters alongside the meeting place which was now filled with people. I went in there with the few Chinese Bibles that I had dared to bring along. I asked, "Do you folks still have your Bibles?" They said that because they were in Mongolia it was treated as an autonomous region. Their Bibles were not confiscated. "They do wear out, you know! Besides, all these new people have no Bibles." I gave out the few I had. That news spread like wildfire. I'll never forget the sight of so many arms stretched out, reaching into that room and so many pleading for a Bible. Suddenly a man's head appeared over the roof. There was always someone spying. Soon he made his way inside to demand a copy; but I had given away all I had.

Instead of staying a full week, we beat it out of that place. By evening the whole city would know that old missionaries had returned and we feared the Christians might get into trouble. We caught the train for the city where the mission cemetery was and to the orphanage where my brother and I had stayed plus where Roland grew up. First we were transported by two old jeeps; but the Mongol in charge of us from then on felt that was not good enough for their first outside guests. After a long wait they came with an ancient ambulance to transport us! As we stood looking at the orphanage, Olia asked, "Are any of the orphans still living?" "Can you give me any names?" the Mongol leader of our party asked. She mentioned two names. An older man, walking toward us, said, "Oh, I know them and I know where they live!" Where? He couldn't tell us but he could show us the way; so he was invited to join our ambulance brigade.

I showed him Dad's picture. "That's your father? Oh, he was a great shot. I used to go hunting with him in the mountains! I'm the pastor in this town. We have between five and six hundred Christians here. Your father had preached in all the towns along this railroad track and in every town there is a thriving church today!"

MOTHER'S GRAVE

We asked to see the old mission cemetery. The Mongol said that he'd take us to the country area and the local farmers would know where it is. All cemeteries had been destroyed years ago. In this case the soil had been used to make brick.

We found the cemetery strewn with bones on top of the ground. I said to the Mongol, "One of these could be my mother!" He felt bad. He said, "We wanted to bring you a good time and now we bring you pain!" I think that he may have feared punishment for bringing us there. We hastened to explain to him that when we Christians die, we go to heaven; so it doesn't matter so much about our bones. Although I would not care to go back there again, I am glad that I went there and saw the place because it was a kind of closure for me.

At the next town we visited where my dad used to preach. A small group of about ten Christians had met secretly for nearly ten years for prayer. They didn't dare to sing because neighbors were all spying on each other. As they met for secret fellowship, they were never caught. When Nixon helped to open China and policies were changed, they asked the government for permission to build a church. He said that when permission was given, "we build this church with our own hands in seven days!" They were also using some homes for these meetings.

FOLLOW-UP FIVE YEARS LATER

Five years later I had another opportunity to return there with Christian literature for the Chinese churches. I brought the only two Mongolian Bibles that I was able to find. The pastor remembered that Mongolian lady he baptized. "Since she sings folk songs for the government and moves from place to place, she has no Christian fellowship and no Bible to read. She has left the Lord; but we have much call for these Mongolian Bibles."

Those original 10 Christians had then grown to 10,000 Christians with 30 churches besides many house churches. We visited their churches going from one to another on a weekday afternoon. I asked one pastor, "How many were here today?" He said, "Over 300 inside but many more outside that couldn't get in." They told us that they pray for the American church every day. I asked, "What do you pray for us?" They

said, "That the affluence won't turn your hearts
from God!"

On my third and last visit four years later, I found
that those original 10 Christians had now grown to
28,000 members with over 70 churches. What was their
secret? The Christians met each morning at 6:00 a.m.
for prayer. I attended such a prayer meeting. Over a
thousand believers gathered for the 6:00 a.m. prayer
before going to work. This was their devotional time in
lieu of no Bibles.

"As soon as we get a church built, it is too small.
Now we are building one to hold 2,500 people. About
150 of our believers come each day to build. On
cement-pouring days between 500 and 600 come." We
attended that weekend on a cement-pouring day. They
were pouring for the balcony. They had only a small
cement mixer. The rest was hand labor. I saw an 80
year-old lady shoveling gravel into the cement mixer.
Two bucket brigades sent the cement in small aluminum
pans, one shovelful of cement to a pan, up the scaffold
to pour cement. One line brought the empty pans down
where a group of women examined them for holes.
These they patched with old aluminum coke cans!
While the cement mixer turned, the choir practiced;
then it was back to building.

Yes, God is building His church and no
government or political party can stop Him. The
estimated 700,000 Christians in China when the
missionaries were driven out are now closer to 90 or

100 million at this writing. There are more Chinese Christians than members of the Communist Party. Praise God for who He is and what He has done.

Ps. 90: 15-17

15. Make us glad for as many days as you have afflicted us, for as many years as we have seen trouble.
16. May your deeds be shown to your servants, your splendor to their children. 17. May the favor of the Lord our God rest upon us; establish thou the work of our hands for us -- yes, the work of our hands, establish thou it.

THAILAND

In 1994 during Evangel Seminary's Christmas holidays, I flew to Thailand with several others representing our Chinese mission board. The visit gave us a clearer understanding of the difficulties our two missionary units faced there.

First the Thai language is especially difficult to master. Just learning people's surnames was hard. No two persons could hold the same surname. Each must be unique resulting in incredibly long names. Demonic power held the Thai people captive. For protection each home had their own "Spirit house" that looked like bird feeders on posts in their back yard. There they offered food daily to appease the demons. The Thai culture seemed to facilitate a demonic stronghold which compounded the work load of our missionaries.

I was amazed to hear that there was a strong Chinese church among them! The Chinese wanted our missionaries to come and minister to THEM. Of course it would be much easier to preach in Chinese; but our missionaries had come to reach the Thai, an unreached people group. I was appalled to hear that the Chinese church in Thailand had no vision or burden to reach the Thai people around them although they knew the Thai language well. Isn't this a picture of our American churches that are too blind to reach out to the multicultural people groups around us?

AUSTRALIA

From Thailand I flew on to Sydney, Australia, where I visited with many special Chinese friends from years back, spoke at two meetings, did some training in Inductive Bible study, and took a week's vacation.

One Chinese family that I stayed with, who were old Living Springs friends from Hong Kong, lived in Griffith an hour inland from Sydney. They requested, "Could you please recruit a Chinese worker to help us start a Chinese church here? " There was no space problem here but just a tragic shortage of trained Chinese pastors.

While in Thailand, I heard that oranges were an out-of-reach luxury there. I kept this in mind the following week on my trip to Australia where I stayed with a Chinese family who had an orange grove! Since my return flight would stop back in Thailand, my

Chinese friends in Australia sent with me two cases of oranges for our Thailand missionaries! Never mind that I had to take them as carry-on luggage. You can imagine the surprise and delight of our Thai missionaries.

I had long wished to visit Australia, to pet a kangaroo, cuddle a Koala bear, to see the Australian Outback and some Aborigines. I didn't dare to dream that all those wishes would be fulfilled beyond expectation in just my one week there!

Even more important, I wanted to visit old friends from Hong Kong who had emigrated there, like former Living Springs youth. It would likely be my last chance to ever see them and catch up on all that God has been doing in their lives. One of these was Samuel whose restaurant started the first of our four Evangelical Free Churches in Sydney.

Actually, I did meet some English speaking CHRISTIAN aborigines. Thanks to missionary work among them, many are now warm hearted Christians. Those I saw were exceedingly black, but their faces shone with the glory of the Lord. Because some missionaries had been available to God to go to the Outback, today many Aborigines are vibrant Christians. In contrast, I was told, as late as 1929, the Australian government sold bow and arrow hunting licenses to HUNT Aborigines for sport!

I had a lovely surprise on my return flight to Hong Kong. My plane was rerouted via Melbourne, so we flew over Australia for six hours, Southeast to Northwest, in mostly clear weather. It gave me an unexpected aerial view of much of the Australian Outback.

On that long, roundabout flight back to Hong Kong, I was weary. "Please, Lord, I'm not so available today." The lady seated by me on that last stretch was from Bhutan (near Nepal). She had gone to a Christian school in India, spoke beautiful English and had a hungry heart. While we ate together, she asked me my religion. She said her husband's family were Christians and often spoke to her of Jesus. She was another prepared heart! In spite of me, before our plane touched down in Hong Kong, God opened her heart to believe and pray to receive Christ! What a blessed climax to that Christmas holiday trip! Since the Bhutan lady was only to be in Hong Kong overnight, I had to do some quick follow-up that afternoon. I returned to my seminary teaching energized to prepare more workers for the ripe harvest.

SINGAPORE

An organization calling itself the Keen Teens Crusade was recruiting Christian youth to train in evangelism. They would participate in an evangelistic crusade, targeting a newly developed suburb of Singapore. Although Singapore's population is mostly Chinese, English is their primary language. Thus the team would be composed of both Chinese and Caucasian youth. Keen Teens used a unique approach to train teens to naturally talk about Jesus and share their faith. By this united evangelistic effort of time spent in training, prayer and mutual sharing, the teens were equipped, energized and empowered for witness.

Keen Teen's strategy was to map out a section of the city, train and send out Christian youth to survey the area home by home. Besides the typical survey questions about family size, ages, schooling, race, etc., this survey would include questions on their religious preferences which led to openings for sharing Christ and personal testimonies. Each family was given an invitation to the evening's lively music, testimonies and messages in the local high school. There they could get their spiritual questions answered and find help toward knowing God.

This effort piqued my interest because our Singapore Evangelical Free Church had just purchased a house in that area for starting a new church plant. Since this was summer vacation at Evangel Seminary, I was free to join that survey team in Singapore for this evangelistic outreach to give a significant boost to our new church plant there. The Keen Teens leader got permission to use the local high school for our headquarters. The school building facilitated both training sessions and prayer times. The auditorium suited our evening evangelistic meetings and a couple of classrooms served for dormitories where we slept on the floor that week with the teens.

We found the suburban residents to be friendly and open to answer survey questions from the young people. The questions and discussions sparked spiritual interest, so many came to the evening evangelistic meetings. Some made lifetime decisions for Christ. Others began a sincere search for God via the Scriptures and our Evangelical Free Church. The team members were challenged and eager to share their faith and excited to see God move in lives. Those teens made themselves available to God; therefore God used them to make an impact beyond their years. Today that church plant they helped to boost is a thriving church reaching far beyond that suburb.

I was interested to observe this unique approach to church planting as well as a means of training youth in evangelism. I always welcome opportunities to introduce people to Jesus; but this was more than a chance to lead individuals to Christ. It was the blessing of being part of a team getting a church started that would continue to reach that suburb. The survey information was invaluable to that new church plant for follow-up, both of the new converts as well as those who had indicated various levels of spiritual interest. Seed was sown, the Gospel was preached, teens were trained and doors were opened for further visits by the church planters. I counted this a valuable learning experience for me, too. While this approach proved a real boost to a church plant in Singapore with its single family dwellings, it would not work in Hong Kong where usually hundreds of people occupy each building. Each setting and culture requires its own approach to church planting and training.

MALAYSIA

Since Singapore was adjacent to Malaysia, I wanted to get up to Kuala Lumpur (KL), the capital of Malaysia, while I was so close.

I knew of a large Christian bookstore there boasting a wide outreach to the rest of Southeast Asia. I wanted to introduce the lovely Go Ye Fellowship gospel plaques to this bookstore. They were available in both English and Chinese and in aluminum or rubber molds to make your own. I believe it can be a significant testimony for Christian homes to have a Gospel plaque on their wall. It can be a conversation opener to talk about Jesus. I was eager to get that testimony on a wall of every Christian home in Malaysia for a silent witness. It was illegal to talk to a Malay about Christianity unless he opened the subject. A gospel plaque could provide such an opening so I was highly motivated to get to Kuala Lumpur. How to do that was the problem.

For years terrorists had roamed the forests of Malaysia. Whether willingly or not, the village people had fed and supported them; so the government had herded the villagers into fenced-in "New Villages," which government forces could monitor and control to dry up the terrorist's activities. This made the terrorists desperate and dangerous so only the fenced-in villages were safe. When I went to Singapore, the New Villages had been opened for about a year. How safe was it now? There was no public transportation available from Singapore to Kuala Lumpur and I had no car. I found a young missionary gal who wanted to visit Kuala Lumpur; but because she didn't know the language, she had feared to drive it alone. She welcomed the chance to drive me there although her tires were poor. We asked each of our four missionary kids there to pray for one tire!

It wasn't the tires that first gave out. Just after we had left Singapore and crossed the Strait of Johore into Malaysia, our car started to jump like a frog and then it stopped dead! When we looked under the car, it appeared that the car's insides had fallen out! (Mechanics would call that the drive shaft!) What could we do in that unfamiliar jungle of Malaysia, far from anywhere? Furthermore, my ship was scheduled to return from Singapore to Hong Kong in just three days. I suggested the other gal stay with her car to guard it. I would thumb a ride into the next village to seek a mechanic's help. We prayed that I could find a Cantonese speaking mechanic! I did.

The two Chinese mechanics explained that it would take three days to fix the car. That's all the time we had. By faith we told them to go ahead. We then thumbed rides for the rest of the way, not knowing how long it would take or where we would spend our nights. We rode mostly with Indian drivers whose driving kept our knuckles white! In each village we found a single missionary lady, available to demonstrate Christ's love to that village and to put us up for the night.

We did find that large bookstore in KL being run by missionaries with wide contacts. Furthermore they shared my vision for the plaque ministry and welcomed the samples I had brought all the way from Hong Kong hoping for this opportunity. When the bookstore manager asked my name, he said "Ekblad is not a common name. I used to do the taxes for a Paul Ekblad in Minneapolis." What a small world! Paul was my brother. That was a delightful surprise God threw my way! We also met other delightful missionaries that day. They blessed our lives before we thumbed our way back, found another village and a missionary who put us up for a night and we found our car all fixed. We were just in time to catch my ship back to Hong Kong.

Count if you will the number of uncertainties we faced on this visit to KL. It was risky in so many ways. Would we get the needed rides? How long would it take to reach KL this way? Could we trust the strangers we thumbed rides with? Would our car still be there and fixed on time? Since we were there on God's business, we just needed to be available. He handled all the uncertainties perfectly!

I need to add that there was a price to pay on the return trip. The South China Sea is notoriously rough. Yes, I did get seasick. Clearly others had gotten sick before me and the cleanup had not been adequate. I had to shuffle my feet to keep the cockroaches off. (This was NOT a cruise ship!) The captain was a jolly, slap-happy fellow. He assured me that he had never lost a passenger yet from sea sickness! He told of one passenger of his that he found standing one evening at the railing feeding the fish. To take passenger's mind off his nausea, the captain changed the subject, saying "Look at that beautiful moon coming up." The passenger replied, "Oh, is THAT coming up, too?"

Being available to God is not rose strewn pathways all our lives through. But what a joy to rely on Him as my competent travel agent!

Chapter 8

THE MONGOLIAN BIBLE AND THE TRANS-SIBERIAN TRIP

TAPESTRY INTRODUCED

God had Moses record the story of how He led the Children of Israel across the Arabian Desert and eventually to the Promised Land. That story of God's marvelous leading by a pillar of cloud by day which shaded them from the hot desert sun and a pillar of fire by night to light their way inspires our faith today. As God led them then, He will lead us today also in protecting, providing and directing us. He is not just a God of long ago. He is active in our lives today. By sharing with one another current examples of His incredible care, our faith is strengthened. Here are a few of my examples of His marvelous leading which I have witnessed in the Far East. May these stories recounted here strengthen your faith and glorify God.

I find that sometimes minor random events that seemed so insignificant at the time would later be revealed as threads to what God was weaving into a marvelous, awesome tapestry.

As I mentioned before, I spent three childhood years from age 3 to 6 in North China, the part called "Inner Mongolia", where my parents were missionaries to the **Chinese**. China's policy toward the territories that they had taken had been to flood the area with ethnic Chinese and so dilute the local culture to make it truly CHINESE.

Therefore, Chinese people filled the cities of Inner Mongolia where my parents served while the nomadic Mongols lived out beyond the mountains on the pasturelands with their herds and moveable yurt-tents. The Mongols had a different language and culture from the Chinese.

WEDDING IN MONGOLIA

When I was a child there, I remember the excitement in our home when Stuart Gunzel, a young missionary colleague of my father, broke the news. He was about to welcome his fiancé from the United States who was coming out to the grasslands of Inner Mongolia to check it out before committing herself to become Stuart's bride and co-worker. In spite of the bleak prospect of isolation as a missionary wife on the Mongolian pasture lands, Margaret said "Yes." She was available.

Margaret came from a prosperous Chicago home and brought to Mongolia her fine wedding gifts, damask tablecloths, fine dishes, etc., little realizing what Mongolia was **really** like. Very soon robbers raided the Gunzel's yurt and made off with ALL her wedding gifts! In spite of this devastating loss and many adjustment tears, Margaret remained available for God to use in Inner Mongolia.

Together Stuart and Margaret labored to win the nomadic Mongols to Christ. Stuart studied the difficult Mongolian language with a Mongol palace prince in exchange for teaching him English. For a time the Gunzels lived on the grasslands in a typical Mongolian yurt which is a moveable tent. This allowed them to follow the nomads and herds to new pastures. Later they moved into a Chinese house. It was available because it was considered haunted!

There were no roads, no stores of any kind up there on the barren pasture lands, no electricity, no phones, no radios or newspapers, no post office or mail service or other English speakers. They were cut off from the outside world. Since the Mongols feared digging into the ground would release evil spirits, there were no garden vegetables or fruit available to vary their staple daily diet of mutton and goat cheese. A river was their only source of water and camels their only transportation. In spite of such harsh conditions, the Gunzels continued to offer themselves to God as AVAILABLE to reach the Mongols for Christ. Under those conditions, their babies were born, their family raised and their children at first home schooled but later sent away for schooling.

The Gunzels, who served under the same TEAM mission as my folks, were close friends of our family.

Periodically my Dad would bring them needed supplies from the capital city where we lived. On those trips we traveled together as a family, via Dad's 1927 Chevy touring car, over the mountains to the pasture lands of Inner Mongolia. From those trips to the grasslands, I grew to love the Mongols almost as much as I loved the Chinese.

GUNZELS REVISE THE MONGOLIAN BIBLE

Let's look at another thread in that tapestry. Nearly twenty years later in 1953, I returned to the Orient as an adult missionary, now twenty three years old. By then, China and Inner Mongolia were under Communist rule and closed to missionary work. I fulfilled my childhood call to tell the Chinese of Jesus by going instead to the British owned colony of Hong Kong.

That first year I lived like Robinson Crusoe on Cheung Chau Island as I studied the Cantonese language. About 30,000 Chinese lived in the village below on the waterfront but I couldn't communicate with them. At that time only one Western family was living on that island with whom I could talk in English. Guess who? Mr. & Mrs. Stuart Gunzel whom I had known as a child in Inner Mongolia as we brought supplies to them on the grasslands! What a treat and special gift from God!

LITERARY VERSION

Although by 1953 with both China and Mongolia closed to missionaries, Stuart Gunzel had in those twenty years studied, learned and become quite a scholar of the Mongolian language. On Hong Kong's dumbbell shaped Island of Cheung Chau, Stuart, with four Mongol scholars, had been working for years to revise the entire Mongolian New Testament.

When I first arrived in Hong Kong, the revision project was completed and Stuart and Margaret Gunzel were preparing to return to Canada. They and the Mongolian scholars had produced a fine revised literary version of the Mongolian New Testament. This literary revision will always be treasured as a literary gem among the educated Mongols. In Stuart's early missionary days, the only Mongols who could read were the monks and they read only literary Mongolian.

The Hong Kong Bible Society printed 8,000 copies of the 1953 newly revised literary version after which the Gunzels returned to Canada. Through them I was quickly introduced to Jergal, the Christian wife of one of those four Mongolian scholars. My friendship with Jergal has continued for years and became one thread in the on-going story of the Mongolian Bible.

REVISITING COMMUNIST CHINA

Another strand in that tapestry was my return in 1982 with several old missionaries to China who wanted to visit Inner Mongolia with me. By this time I had been a missionary in Hong Kong almost thirty years. China was just beginning to open to Chinese tourists from the outside world. Since President Nixon's visit to China in 1972, China's political policies had changed. Christians, who had been worshipping secretly in fear, were emboldened to ask for permission to build a church. At one place we visited, the Christians said, "When permission was granted, we built this church with our own hands in 7 days!"

MONGOLIAN LADY BAPTIZED

In my former home city, we visited where the church met. It was a one story residential building with room dividers knocked out to form a small sanctuary that was packed with people. The church-yard was filled with their bicycles. The morning service was followed by an afternoon baptismal service.

In the chapter "Return to Mongolia" I mentioned that among the 43 believers baptized that day was a Mongolian lady. Her words, "I understand spoken Mandarin but I can't read Chinese. Is there such a thing as a Mongolian Bible?" I promised that I would try to find one for her. Now to see where that promise led!

Upon my return from Inner Mongolia to Hong Kong, I went to find Jergal, my Mongolian friend. Because of her burden for her own people, Jergal had scoured South East Asia for any copies left of the 8,000 Mongolian New Testaments that missionary Gunzel, with Jergal's husband (now deceased) and the other

Mongol scholars had revised and printed thirty years before. Jergal had given the few copies she had found to Mongolian friends who had come down to Hong Kong for business or to visit her. She said, "I have just two copies left beside my own copy and the one copy that I have saved for reprinting. " She gave me the two she had available. I was determined to get back to my home city in Inner Mongolia to bring a copy to that Mongolian lady who was baptized that Sunday and requested one.

Five years passed before I could fulfill that dream to go back. In 1987, I had my second opportunity to return to Inner Mongolia. I brought along Chinese Bibles and Christian literature for the Chinese Christians there. We were always fearful of getting caught by the X-ray machines that checked our baggage as we cleared customs. I also brought along those two Mongolian New Testaments that Jergal had given me for that Mongolian lady who requested one back in 1982. The Chinese pastor there remembered the Mongolian lady that he had baptized. He said, "She has a lovely singing voice so her job for the government is to sing Mongolian folk songs to Chinese tourists. The result was she was moved about from place to place. With no Christian fellowship and no Bible to read, she had backslidden and left the Lord; but I have many requests for Mongolian Bibles," he said. With a heavy heart, I left those two copies of the Mongolian New Testament with that Pastor.

NAGGING BURDEN

When I returned to Hong Kong, I found Jergal, my Mongolian friend, and told her the sad story and the urgent need for getting that Mongolian New Testament reprinted. What a shame! After all the work of getting it revised and printed, and such a beautiful revision at that, here it was out of print and unavailable! We prayed together about it and then went to the Hong Kong Bible Society to plead for a reprint. We were asked, "What are your prospects for distribution to Mongolia?" We had no answer. The country was tightly sealed. Any luggage we might bring in would go through an X-ray machine checking for literature. What's the use of reprinting it just to store it in Hong Kong?

Months slipped by, but Jergal and I could not drop our nagging burden for getting that New Testament reprinted. She had been back up country and seen the spiritual hunger there. This time Jergal and I made an appointment with Ms. Violet Wong, then head of the Hong Kong Bible Society, with whom we shared our burden. She asked the same question, "What are your prospects for distribution?" This time Jergal replied differently. She said, "I've been back up into Mongolia and I've seen firsthand the spiritual hunger there. If I had 10,000 copies up there, there'd be such a demand that they would just go SWISH." Violet Wong answered, "Then we must do it." Jergal said, "I know where the blocks are safely stored that were used to print it 35 years ago." Violet Wong said, "No, we don't print that way anymore. We use offset now. We photograph each page to make a copy on plastic for offset printing." She calculated the number of pages and concluded that it would cost $2,000.00 (U.S. money) just to do the offset preparation for printing. "We don't have that kind of money on hand but let's pray it in!" And we did!

Another strand to that tapestry was the contact I'd had with an organization in the United States, the Wayfarers, who just loved to raise funds to donate to unique missionary projects! I contacted them. They raised the $2,000.00 for offset photography. This way would make future reprints much simpler and cheaper.

I contacted friends and supporting churches for the funds to re-print by offset. Eventually, in 1988 we had the needed funds for the Bible Society to re-print another 2,000 copies of the "1953 literary revision". The copies could be given out free. To get them into China more easily, they couldn't look like Bibles; so we chose a plain rust color for the hard covers with India paper.

Even the first "Gunzel revision", printed 35 years earlier, which Jergal had saved for reprinting, though never used, just fell apart when it was opened. It was held together by cheesecloth binding which had rotted in Hong Kong's humid heat. Therefore, I insisted that these Bibles be bound with nylon material and have hard covers. The printer wasn't happy about that because their machines couldn't handle the nylon. They had to be bound by hand! I said, "They must last until the Lord comes!"

ACROSS SIBERIA

Now enters another strand of that tapestry. A German mission to the Mongols would cooperate with us. This mission found a way to smuggle these Mongolian New Testaments into Inner Mongolia but by a very circuitous route! They had first to be boxed and shipped from Hong Kong to Christian friends in Germany. Because East Germany had been allied with Russia during the war and Outer Mongolia was under Russian control, goods from Germany were not tightly checked at the Outer Mongolia-Siberia border. The boxes of Mongolian New Testaments were loaded into trucks in Germany and hidden behind loads of used clothes for the poor in Mongolia. The trucks also hauled legitimate medical supplies and donated school supplies for the poor children in Mongolia. These trucks had to travel all the way across Siberia to Russian Outer Mongolia and then travel south from Outer Mongolia to Inner Mongolia where they could be discreetly distributed! This was a long slow, expensive route but the precious cargo was well worth it! The German Mongol mission handled this.

I need to clarify here that although Inner Mongolia had continued using their own written script, the Russians had forbidden Outer Mongolia, which they controlled, to write using the traditional Mongolian script. Instead Outer Mongolia had to write using the

Russian alphabet! By this time after 40 years of Russian rule, the 2 million population of Outer Mongolia had lost the use of their own written language. The spoken language of Inner and Outer Mongolia remained the same. Our Mongolian testaments were printed in the traditional Mongolian script which was still used by the 6 million population of Inner Mongolia. Since 1991 when Outer Mongolia became independent of Russia, the old Mongolian script has been gradually re-introduced in the schools of Outer Mongolia. Thus, the upcoming generation there will also be able to read these testaments.

SUMMERS STATE-SIDE

Now for another seemingly unrelated incident that God was weaving into this picture. In the 1980s it was getting increasingly difficult for me to cope with the summer heat and humidity of Hong Kong. I was on home assignment in 1981 and when I was speaking at a combined Sunday school at the Willmar, Minnesota Evangelical Free Church, someone asked this question, "What is the most difficult thing for you to cope with in Hong Kong?" That was easy to answer. I had even been wondering how much longer I would be able to continue working in Hong Kong due to my body's reaction to those unbearable summers. That evening the church board approached me with an offer. "Our church is growing so fast. Many of these people have had no exposure to missions before. You communicate with our people. We would love to bring you home each summer. Since your Evangel Seminary where you are teaching is in recess anyway and you could take your vacation, you could give our church a week or two and then do deputation for your seminary. That airfare would cost just a fraction of what we're already paying for INTEREST on our church building!" Thus, the Lord opened the way for me to return to the United States each summer thereafter for another fifteen plus years.

One summer, while I was participating in a mission's conference at a church in a Midwestern city, it was arranged for me to speak to a fellowship of Chinese students at the university there. After the meeting a Chinese couple came up to ask questions and to speak with me. They were deeply stirred by the Gospel. Could it really be true? The wife, for security reasons, I'll call her "Hannah," said "I was once such a convinced Communist that I reported my own father to the government. He was arrested and imprisoned. After ten years in prison, he hung himself there. Later when I realized how false the Communist ideology is, I became so disillusioned; I never dared to trust anything again. I couldn't stand it if I put my trust in God and then found that He was false. That would disillusion me again." For two consecutive summers I visited that church and the university's Chinese fellowship and spent hours again with this Chinese couple who was studying there and still wrestling with the claims of Christ. Little did I realize that they were eventually to become my very close friends and a significant link to my ministry in China and Mongolia!

INTELLIGENTSIA BELIEVED

A couple years later while I was teaching in Hong Kong, I received a letter from Hannah in China, asking how she could qualify to become a student in my school! She knew it was a seminary. What was she trying to tell me? Did she want to become a Christian? The intelligentsia in China was closely watched. Our mail would be censored. I wrote back that my schedule for the year was full but I would give priority the following year to travel to China to visit her. When I did, her first words to me, before she'd even gotten off her bike, were, "Now I belong to Jesus!" She had been sent by the Chinese government to Australia to give a science lecture. There she found Christian Chinese who helped her to trust Christ! "What about your husband?" I asked. "I don't think that he feels the need"; but in their flat, while she was fixing food in the kitchen, I asked her husband, "What do you think of Jesus?" He answered, "I believe but I must be like Peter and deny my Lord. If the government knew that I am a Christian, I'd lose my job as professor in a university here." He did not deny Christ in word. He just never mentioned it not even to his wife, until our meal together that evening. Eventually he found a way to send his key students, one at a time, to Australia to study for a year under a Christian professor in his specialized field. Invariably, the students returned as Christians. Thereafter, this couple's home became my base of operations when I had errands in their city. I even kept my own bicycle there for transportation!

TRANS-SIBERIAN TRAIN

My father, in 1917, had first traveled from Sweden to China by the Trans-Siberian train, rolling 18 days and nights while sitting on hard benches. I had dreamed of taking that same Trans-Siberian train trip myself someday as I returned to the United States by way of Mongolia, Russia and Europe. I hoped thereby to bring a world vision to my Evangel Seminary students in Hong Kong and find some prepared hearts along the way to introduce to Jesus. I also wanted to spread news of Jergal's daily Mongolian gospel broadcasts via Far East Broadcasting Company (FEBC) of Hong Kong. With the added incentive of distributing the reprinted Mongolian Bible, these plans came together. I made plans to return to the United States that summer of 1991, which included traveling alone via the Trans-Siberian train.

I bought my ticket from the "Monkey Business Travel Service" in Hong Kong. It cost just (U.S.) $150.00 to travel from Beijing across Mongolia and Siberia to Moscow but you would travel at your own risk.

First I needed to get my Mongolian visa from Beijing at a very remote and hardly accessible hotel. It was a real flophouse. The Canadian in-charge groaned at the conditions. He told me, "We have a continual turnover of help here. I have to explain to each new worker how to run a vacuum sweeper and why they can't use the same rag that they used to wipe out the

toilet to wipe out the room's drinking glasses!"
Fortunately, I did not have to spend even one night in
that flophouse with who knows how many bugs! A
young fellow that I had mentored from my Living
Springs Sunday School class in Hong Kong had insisted
on paying for a room for me in a very posh hotel in
that city.

After getting my visa at the flophouse, at
daybreak the next morning, I pulled my suitcases filled
with clothes, food, and forty hard-covered Mongolian
Bibles through a mob of people at the station. I boarded
my train that was nicknamed "Iron Rooster". It ran from
Beijing across Inner and Outer Mongolia to the Russian
border and onward. Sixteen of us had bought from the
Monkey Business Travel Service this packaged trip
from Beijing to Moscow, across Siberia, Poland and
Germany to Amsterdam.

The trip included stops at two camps in Outer
Mongolia. All of us who bought that train ticket for that
week became a sort of tour group. Young British,
Australian, French, Swiss and American youth between
college and graduate school, trying to find themselves,
were backpacking through China, India, Tibet, Nepal
and now Mongolia and Siberia! They were wary of
having this missionary among them. "Like having your
MOTHER along," one of them said between drinks.
They were young and helpful to me with my heavy
luggage. Four hard shelves per compartment served as
our bunk beds. We were traveling economy class
for sure.

GOSPEL BROADCASTS

Our train was full of Mongols who had filled their cabins with enormous sacks of cheap Beijing clothes to sell at train stops along the way. The Russians had money but few products to buy. At the train stops in Russia, these passengers, from the train windows, would argue prices as they made sales with the crowds at each stop.

Upon our arrival at Ulan Bator, the capital of Outer Mongolia, we were whisked off by bus to a campsite nestled in a picturesque valley among spruce covered hills where we slept one night in a Mongolian yurt. This was part of our package deal. I had hoped for some ministry opportunity in Mongolia. I found more than I asked for!

I had a few hundred Xeroxed notices that gave both time and frequency of the daily Mongolian Gospel broadcasts. I wanted to make these broadcasts more widely known. The broadcasts were prepared and recorded by Jergal, my Christian Mongolian friend, and were beamed by Far East Broadcasting Company (FEBC) from the Philippines. Jergal had written these notices which I had duplicated in quantity to hand out. Unfortunately, the people of Outer Mongolia couldn't read their own traditional Mongolian script. They could neither read these notices nor could they read the New Testaments that I had brought. Wherever I showed those notices, there was instant excitement. They recognized it as their own language but they struggled in vain to read it. One lady at the camp, who knew both the Mongolian script and the Russian alphabet writing, took my stack of leaflets and copied by hand the same message in the Russian alphabet on the back of each leaflet. Now I could communicate news of the Gospel broadcasts to ANY Mongol.

Around one camp there were yurts for tourists, a dozen small wooden huts for the Mongolian staff who ran the camp, and farther away, more Mongolian yurts for the locals. Early the next morning by using sign language to communicate with one family at their yurt, I got myself invited into a yurt for a true Mongolian breakfast. This was fascinating. How would you like to join me there to a bowl of warm horse-milk tea and hard white cheese? Stuck away in that yurt, I found an educated Mongol scholar who had written a book in the old Mongolian script on the plants of Mongolia! He was thrilled to get the New Testament from me and promptly began to read it. By hand signals, he begged me for more copies to give to his Inner Mongolian friends who lived on the other side of that mountain. A welcomed request! That evening at the time of the Mongolian gospel broadcast, I returned to his yurt to see if he was tuned in. I found it packed with Mongols who were sitting on the ground and straining to hear the Gospel on his tiny radio. It was too weak to pick up the signal and Jergal's voice beaming from the Philippines. How tragic! I wanted to weep!

BIG GOOFS

At that camp I pulled a triple blunder. I lost my bag of 3,000 Chinese characters that I had along for review on the trip besides my Chinese Bible. I had left these briefly at a pagoda while I was taking a picture of the camp when the afternoon sun hit it just right. Those character cards were hand done and irreplaceable. I wanted to review them on this week-long train ride. Assuming that my bag had been stolen, our English speaking Mongol tour guide made me go with him to each yurt and wooden hut around the camp to search for the thief. I was impressed with how clean and neat each place was. I let my tour guide do the talking. I thought, obviously, they're never going to admit taking my stuff! After we'd made the rounds, he told me that they were all angry with me now for accusing them! He added, "By the way, do you realize that there are two pagodas?" I didn't and we found all my stuff still on the bench at the other pagoda just where I left it! I was mortified! Now I had made enemies by my own stupidity. I had my tour guide teach me how to say in Mongolian, "I lost it. I found it. I'm sorry"! I wrote this in phonetics and practiced saying it right; then I made the rounds again to each hut and yurt and delighted the Mongols with both my Mongolian apology and the bags of candy and gum that I had brought along as apology gifts. Not only did they forgive me, but that goof opened the door to each yurt and hut for me to visit twice, to become their friend and share the news of the gospel broadcasts on leaflets with each home! God's ways beat our plans hands down!

FOOD ON THE JOURNEY

Back in the capital city of Ulan Bator, I sought to prepare for our week long ride across Siberia. I was fortunate to find a market where I could buy eggs that were not rationed. I bought two dozen eggs to boil and share with our group of sixteen who were traveling together. The staff at the camp where our group stayed for several days wanted to boil those eggs for me, but I knew they'd boil them green. I persuaded them to let me boil them in the camp kitchen. When I opened the kitchen fridge to keep the eggs cool, I was aghast. Every shelf inside that fridge was filled with raw mutton, punched in and hanging out against the door. I was proud of our group of college kids for I never heard our kids complain about the food as well they might have. We ate mostly mutton and cheese every day plus tomatoes and cucumbers grown in the local greenhouses. Vegetables were not available in the Mongolia that I knew as a child.

How could I have any ministry to this city beyond our camp when I didn't know the Mongolian language? I found that in the absence of newspapers, bulletin boards were widely used to disseminate information; so I walked many miles around the city those few days to tack the leaflet notices of the Mongolian gospel broadcasts on the public notice boards. Curious crowds would then gather to read my notice and so the good news of the gospel broadcasts spread! I also freely handed out the broadcast notices to individuals, showing first the side written in Mongol script. If the person couldn't read that, I'd just turn the leaflet over. If they could read their own script, I'd hand them a New Testament, too. I was happy to reduce my load of 40 heavy testaments. Each one was the size of a normal hard covered hymn book!

REACHING RUSSIA

The Trans-Siberian trip offered plenty of adventure. To protect themselves from armies which might invade by rail, the Russians had built their railroads with a narrower gauge. This meant every train car had to be jacked up and the wheels removed and exchanged for a new set of wheels to match the Russian rails. After crossing Mongolia, we reached the Russian border at night. There we were all marched off the train for the exchange of wheels. All train doors, including those to the bathrooms, were locked for nine hours during this process. You solve your own problems!

STOLEN PASSPORT

Back on the train, our passports were repeatedly scrutinized by Russian officers. The train compartment next to ours held two Swedish ladies who were fulfilling their lifetime dream of taking the Trans-Siberian "Iron Rooster" from Sweden to Beijing. Now they said, "Never again!" They warned us of multiple dangers.

One of those ladies had her purse and passport stolen one night even though their compartment door was locked! Thieves had used master keys to enter while they slept. Upon reaching the Russian-Mongolian border, Mongol agents there would not permit them to proceed with a missing passport nor would the Russian agents on the train permit them to return to Sweden without a passport! Fortunately, the same Russian officer, who had checked their passports at Moscow, was on board. In the hubbub that followed, he came by, recognized them and permitted them to return by the same train to Moscow to solve their problems with the Swedish consulate there; so we traveled together to Moscow.

We were warned that thieves had skeleton keys to our compartments. There was a small lever one could lower to block the sliding door from opening; but the thieves had long knives to reach in and flip that lever back. To be safe, each night we must tie our door-handle firmly to the ladder for the upper bunk.

DINING CUISINE

The dining car had a fabulous menu but only one dish was actually served. It was goulash served three times a day with the portions growing progressively smaller! At every train stop we would exit to search for food. We never dared to leave our compartment empty at the train stations. One of us must stay on guard. Once it was my turn to be on guard duty at a station and our cabin window was down just four inches from the top. Suddenly a hand reached in that upper window, grabbed my roommate's down sleeping bag and took off with it. The thief ran under the next train which was also standing still. He must have stood on the shoulders of another man to reach in the high window. It all happened so fast. I had no chance to stop them or chase after them. They had timed it right. Just then our train whistle blew so all the passengers must hurry back on board or get left behind! There was no chance to chase after the lost item.

I had brought along a full box of highly prized Wrigley's chewing gum to exchange at train stops for food. Besides bartering for bread, at one train stop I bartered a pack of gum for a deliciously cooked chicken thigh. Another time it was for fresh strawberries that filled a newspaper folded into a cone.

WHISTLE STOPS

At the stops, robbers were known to board, swarm over the train and, at knife-point, rob every passenger of money, pens, watches and valuables; so the train stewardesses had grown smart. Whenever the train stopped at stations and the passengers would disembark, the train staff would let down the platform to cover the train steps. No one could board until the train whistle blew and the cover over the steps was removed; then everyone must re-board. The passengers were checked to verify that each boarding passenger was recognized. At one stop I had wandered far from my car when the whistle blew. I ran to board the nearest car but the stewardess took me for a white Russian. She wouldn't lift the platform to let me on! I screamed as I held to the railings for dear life with one knee up on the

platform. I feared that I would get stranded in Siberia! Just then my car's stewardess came by and recognized me. They both helped to pull me up on board. I was mighty thankful not to be stranded
in Siberia!

MONGOLIAN PROFESSOR

Our train pulled many cars. I walked up and down those cars and met many people. Among them, unknown to me, was another thread to God's tapestry. It was a professor of the Mongolian language from a university in Beijing. He knew the old Mongolian script so I went back to my cabin to get him a copy of the literary Mongolian New Testament. He later came back to find me and asked, "Could I have ten more copies? I want to use them as textbooks in my university classes!" I was delighted to unload ten more heavy copies from my suitcase! To think that the Mongolian New Testament would be used in a tightly controlled Beijing university as a text book right under the nose of the atheistic Communist government! Praise God for that victory! I never asked the professor his name. Little did I realize how significant he would become in God's tapestry of the Mongolian Bible or ten years later I would be hunting for him without knowing his name, his university or his address! That will be another story.

MOSCOW EXPERIENCE

I was warned that at the train station in Moscow, gypsy kids would swarm around passengers, laughing, waving their arms and closing in to rob passengers of money belts, fanny packs or purses. You couldn't hit them. They were just children who were trained to do this. When our train stopped at Moscow's main station, I stepped out right into the arms of one of our Hong Kong missionary kids! An answer to prayer! Blair Carlson, whom I had known as a baby, was now grown and my host in Moscow. He had worried how he would find me on that very long train! He was in Moscow with his family for a year, laying the groundwork to prepare for the upcoming Billy Graham crusade there. He provided me with an English-speaking tour guide who took me around the city, Red Square and all. As we talked together, she voiced a definite spiritual hunger. As we sat on a park bench right under a large statue of Lenin, I explained the simple gospel to her. There, with a ready heart, she believed and sincerely put her trust in Jesus as her Savior. (Lenin must have turned over in his grave). Later she invited me to her home in Moscow to meet her family and explain the gospel to them, too. She was the first of seven prepared hearts that God led me to on that trip who were ready, when they heard the Gospel, to pray to invite Christ into their lives. I was on cloud nine. Surely, God led me on that trip to pick ripe fruit for Him.

There were other adventures in Moscow. On several mornings of the week that I was there, I joined the morning devotional time for the workers who were preparing the logistics of the Graham campaign. It was not possible to find many Christians for this. After sharing with them one morning and giving my testimony, one of them later that day wanted to talk and prayed to receive Christ. One Christian on the Graham team, hearing that I was a seminary teacher, begged, "Could you give me in a few hours a crash course in seminary?"

I found many Chinese in Moscow whom I invited to the Graham crusade. If I could find enough interest among them, the crusade would add Chinese interpretation to Graham's messages! Day after day I went through the market to walk behind Oriental looking persons and to ask softly in Chinese, "Are you Chinese?" If they were, they would whirl around and speak with me. If not, they wouldn't hear it. Among the Orientals there were Mongols, Koreans, Japanese, Vietnamese and Chinese. During that week in Moscow, I had some good social times with the Chinese that I met there but I found little spiritual interest among them. Only God can prepare hearts.

RESCUED BY A STRANGER

It was time to leave my good friends, the Blair Carlson family, and proceed to cross Europe. My train ticket should have taken me all the way from Moscow to Holland, but for some unexplained reason, I was bumped off that train at some large train station in Russia while the train sped on, leaving me stunned and stranded on the train platform. I didn't know why or in what city I was in. The conductor could not speak English or explain why I was bumped. I knew no Russian. The conductor's gestures left me wondering if he wanted more money. Did this train have sleepers and my ticket didn't cover that? I was bewildered. I was alone somewhere in Siberia with no contacts and no place to go for help! My traveler's checks were useless there. As my train sped off, I knew only to pray.

Just then I noticed a slender young black lady on my same platform who was apparently awaiting another train. As she turned towards me, I observed that she was stunningly beautiful, simply dressed and wearing a dark green coat. Not only did she impress me, she looked straight at me and came walking directly toward me. With outstretched arm and without a word, she handed me a crisp (U.S.) twenty dollar bill!

I was dumbfounded! Why did she do this? She was a total stranger. How did she know that I needed cash? At that moment the next train pulled in. Its engine noise drowned out any possible conversation. I had no chance to even thank her. I had to board that next train immediately since it was headed the right direction. I handed my ticket and the twenty dollar bill to the conductor. He smiled, welcomed me on board and gave me Russian currency for change. I am still at a loss to understand that black lady's action. Could she have been an angel? She certainly was an answer to my prayer of desperation. Whoever she was, may God reward her!

POLAND, AMSTERDAM AND LONDON

In Poland, I had some unexpected adventures. I had been given an address of a Baptist pastor there. I disembarked at a stop that I understood the conductor to call Poland. There were several stops in Poland and I got off at the wrong one! When I showed the address to the taxi driver, he said he knew the way. He sure took me for a ride—25 miles and expensive! We were hopelessly lost. It was evening when I saw a group of well-dressed people walking together. I made a quick decision, paid off the taxi driver and hurried to join those people. They were Polish/English speaking who were on their way to a Rotary Club meeting! They invited me to accompany them to this Polish meeting after which I could go home with one couple as their guest! The next day they would help me! God's amazing care! Their beautiful home which was set in a lovely wooded area had a separate guest house in their back yard that was fully furnished with hot shower and bed! I had breakfast and a wonderful time with this Polish couple who later drove me back to my train.

Further adventures awaited me with Chinese contacts in Germany, Amsterdam, and London. In Amsterdam, for example, I was blessed to spend time with Honson and Man Ning, a Chinese couple that I had mentored in their high school days. They were in my Living Springs Sunday School class and youth group in Hong Kong. Now Honson worked for Philips Camera Co. to support himself and his family while he served as a lay preacher for several Chinese churches which reached out to the large Chinese population of Amsterdam. What a treat to see God's hand on his life!

In London I was specially blessed. I stayed at the headquarters of the Chinese Christian Mission and enjoyed fellowship with old Chinese friends that I had known in Hong Kong. Although I had only three days in London, I wanted to see the highlights, such as the changing of the guard, Number 10 Downing Street and the Westminster Abbey. I certainly experienced God's favor that day as He arranged those days there beyond belief!

I found my way to the subway train only to discover that the British lady who sat beside me was a secretary to the House of Lords. She explained that this was their last day of session for the House of Lords that season and she invited me to sit in on it as her guest! Wow! After that impressive session, she graciously showed me around the Westminster Abbey, took me to #10 Downing Street and to see the changing of the guards. A large crowd stood outside the fence watching this majestic event. From somewhere in that crowd, I heard my Chinese name called out! "Hui Kwoo Neung, Hui Kwoo Neung." There in that crowd was one of my former Evangel Seminary students now in London with his wife and family! What an unexpected joyous reunion! God sprinkled my path with unexpected delights. A foretaste of heaven!

From London I flew to the United States, completed my week at the Willmar Evangelical Free

Church and my round of meetings with supporting churches. I did promotion work for Evangel Seminary, had some days of vacation with my family in Wisconsin and returned to Hong Kong all within 60 days! I was back just in time for fall classes to begin at Evangel Seminary. God's abundant favor blessed this trip.

A REPRINT NEEDED

Another year, just as I was getting ready to leave for a summer in the United States, I got a phone call from a total stranger. He was in Hong Kong from the United States. "I work for a Korean Christian organization that brings Bibles into China for minority people-groups. These Bibles are printed in their local dialects". His custom was to bring mailbags full of these Scriptures into China. Because the books were not bound to look like Bibles and the border guards couldn't read them, they didn't know that they were Scriptures. The customs agents would just say, "Here comes the man with the books!" He didn't need to go through X-ray baggage checks like I had to. He would just fly with his Scripture portions to various cities in China where he had distribution contacts. His greatest expense was his overweight baggage on the plane!

On the phone he said, "I'm on my way to China. I need 200 copies of the Mongolian Bible by tomorrow and I can't find any more in Hong Kong's Christian bookstores." Certain Christian bookstores in Hong Kong had rooms stacked with free Bibles for China. Plenty of donations came from North America for

Bibles for China, but little for the travel expenses of bringing them in! This brother had already delivered hundreds of copies of our literary Mongolian New Testament and now couldn't find any more! I directed him to the Hong Kong Bible Society which still had a few hundred copies and they were all paid for. Immediately, I had to network with key people to get another 2,000 reprints! Since I was returning to the United States, I could raise funds for the reprinting. This Bible courier requested soft covers next time instead of hard. "They are SO heavy"! Praise God, we did get them reprinted with soft covers and our courier friend was able to bring a significant portion of those 2,000 new reprints into Mongolia before he was caught and deported. Eventually, Christian tourists traveling to China brought a few in at a time until all those reprints were distributed.

COLLOQUIAL TRANSLATION

Gradually feedback came to us that this Mongolian testament which was so literary in style and treasured by the intelligentsia was too difficult for the common people who were now reading colloquial Mongolian. Because the literary translations were out of stock anyway, a colloquial translation of the whole Mongolian New Testament became an obvious need. Jergal, being not only a Christian but also a very gifted Mongol herself who spoke five languages, researched and recommended an exceptionally gifted translator for the job. He had already translated two Old Testament books into colloquial Mongolian for the German

Mongol mission. Genesis was chosen for the creation story and Psalms for its help in worship. Both had to be handwritten as there was no Mongolian computer font available at that time.

Although this translator did not know the original Biblical languages, he carefully compared the literary Mongolian version with Chinese translations plus various English versions. It was a daunting task to re-translate the whole New Testament into colloquial Mongolian and written in the traditional vertical script of Inner Mongolia. Although several other translators were tried, the quality of their Mongolian writing did not meet Jergal's standard. They were soon dropped. This task for one translator took years. (He became a Christian in the process.) Those of us who were burdened for this need were networking with the German Mongol mission on this project.

My involvement was just one small link in the chain of efforts. I was networking, helping to raise prayer support and the funds for translation and printing, finding a publisher, etc. My involvement in this whole project was a sideline to a full teaching schedule in our Evangel Seminary in Hong Kong. My childhood roots in Mongolia drew me to this project like a magnet. Mongolians are great singers. I envisioned the long term effect of this colloquial Mongolian New Testament would lead eventually to throngs of Christian Mongols in heaven swelling the great choir of the redeemed there singing praises to the Lamb!

The colloquial translation was finally completed in the year 2000. We had entrusted the printing of this version to New Life Literature, Hong Kong. They were publishing Scriptures in many languages, especially for the minority people groups in China. As a small organization, their publishing was more cost effective than the Hong Kong Bible Society. They also had them printed in Japan where the best India paper was available.

After my retirement to the United States in 1997, I returned to Hong Kong for speaking engagements in 2001. While there I hoped to find our colloquial Mongolian New Testament already printed by then. Not so. One reason was because the World Bible League who had agreed to fund the print job was short on funds. Furthermore, New Life Literature of Hong Kong, due to a misunderstanding, had doubts about the quality of the Mongolian language used in our new translation. Jergal, who was the Mongolian proof-reader, had referred to the translator as "my brother". (Actually she meant her spiritual brother.) The publisher reasoned that if this work was all done "in house" by Jergal and her brother, of course, she would say it is a beautiful translation! But IS it really? So the Enemy used this misunderstanding to delay the printing another year.

The huge question was how could we from Hong Kong check if this translation was really good Mongolian before spending the money to print it? None of us involved knew the Mongolian language except Jergal. Now when the translation was completed, her testimony was suspect! My time in Hong Kong on this trip was very limited. God help us!

A WILD GOOSE CHASE

We could hardly check the flow of this new colloquial translation with existing Mongolian pastors because of a strong disagreement in the Mongolian church on which name they could use for "God". This issue had split the tiny Mongolian church. Can the traditional term that the Buddhists use for deity be used for our God? Some insisted the term "Master" should be used instead but, according to Jergal, it did not convey the meaning of "deity". We needed to skirt that theological issue since we needed an unbiased evaluation of the writing as good or poor Mongolian. Those of us networking on the project concluded that we should find a non-Christian Mongol scholar to check if this colloquial translation was good Mongolian. Would the common people understand it? Where could we in a short time in Hong Kong find such a neutral Mongol scholar?

I suddenly remembered that Mongol professor that I had met on the Trans- Siberian train ten years before. Unfortunately, I hadn't asked for his name, his address, or his university. I only knew that he taught in a university in Beijing and I had met him on a train in Siberia ten years before! This professor of the Mongolian language would be an ideal authority to evaluate the quality of Mongolian used in this colloquial translation; but how could I find him?

At that time, Beijing had a population of thirteen million. Could the Lord lead me to find that Mongolian professor among thirteen million people since I knew neither name, address, nor the university where he taught?

The flight from Hong Kong to Beijing to find this man to get this translation properly checked would cost me (U.S.) $500.00 round trip. I prayed for some clue from the Lord to know whether this flight to find him was God's will for me. Unless God was in it, this would be only an expensive and foolish wild goose chase.

From Hong Kong I phoned Hannah, my Chinese friend in Beijing, asking her to put a note on the university bulletin board, saying, "The Western lady who met a Mongol professor on the Trans-Siberian train in June ten years ago is coming to Beijing and needs to see him again. Please respond." Hannah asked me, "Which university? There are over a hundred universities in Beijing!" She began to name some. Surely this effort was totally ridiculous; but what if God is in this….? I said, "Try the Peking University." It was one of those she had named. She did.

In the meantime I was busy in Hong Kong, while I waited for word from the Lord on whether I should or should not fly to Beijing. Finally there were just four available days left before the conference for which I had flown to Hong Kong to speak! That Friday afternoon I got a Christmas email from Miss Ma, a Chinese student that I had helped to find Christ at the University of

Minnesota. She wrote that she was then in Beijing working on a thesis project! (She had no idea that I was then in Hong Kong!)

"Thank you Lord. This is my clue from you!" I immediately phoned China Southern Airlines and booked my ticket to Beijing for Monday. Immediately after taking that step of faith, I got another email. This time it was from a Peking University professor who had read my bulletin board note. His email said, "Your note must mean Mr. Ni, our Mongolian professor who took the Trans-Siberian train for Moscow in June ten years ago. He died of stomach cancer this summer but perhaps I can help you! We have a Mongolian department here at this university. I am one of a number of Mongolian professors here!" I made an appointment to meet with him on Tuesday. Then I emailed Miss Ma asking her if she could find and schedule for me an interview with another Mongol scholar of another Beijing university also on Tuesday. I wanted to double check with a second opinion.

Before flying to Beijing, I needed to get a few sample pages of the new translation printed out to bring along for the professors to examine and evaluate for quality. Unfortunately, the New Life Literature office was already closed for the weekend and my flight was for early Monday morning! More problems! Both Miss Ma and the professor that I was to meet emailed me on Saturday to say that they were sick with a bad case of the flu and wouldn't be able to meet me! My plane ticket was for Monday and the two appointments for Tuesday. I proceeded anyway by faith alone.

EXCELLENCE CONFIRMED

Fortunately, the head of New Life Literature had gotten my email request for those sample pages of Luke and John and he had the samples waiting for me at the Hong Kong airport Monday morning! Hannah met my plane in Beijing. Both my contacts, the flu victims, recovered enough to proceed with Tuesday's interviews; but the results from both interviews were devastating. The Mongolian departments of both the Peking University and the University of Eastern Oriental Languages said, "You don't want to print this. It is full of spelling errors!" My heart sank.

Suddenly I remembered that I had a copy of the Mongolian Psalms back at Hannah's flat where I was staying. That had been previously translated by the same translator and was all handwritten because we had no good Mongolian computer font back then. Perhaps these spelling errors were just computer typos instead of a poor translation. Both authorities agreed to meet me again the next day to compare those samples with the handwritten Psalms; but "Meet me in my office." Privacy was important.

When they saw the handwritten Psalms, the authorities of both universities gave thumbs up. "This is BEAUTIFUL Mongolian, even in difficult poetry!" I asked, "Could you correct the typos for us?" Fortunately we were alone. I offered to pay for the job personally. The professor said, "That makes a lot of difference. I am young and you are old. You are doing this for my people; then I cannot charge much. I can only charge you my wages." He tried proofreading several pages and then he calculated. "If there are a thousand pages, it will take a full month to complete it. My university salary, including benefits, is between three and four hundred (U.S.) dollars a month. That's what I would charge you." I said, "It's a deal!"

Actually it turned out to be 1,058 pages. Before returning to the United States, I left my $400.00 with Far East Broadcasting Co. friends who frequent Beijing. They discreetly brought him the documents, paid him and brought the corrected copy back to Hong Kong. Jergal typed those corrections into her computer. Finally by the following year, the whole corrected colloquial Mongolian New Testament was completed on one CD disk which I was able to deliver to the Beijing professor in person as a gift for his University library! Now all we needed was money to print it. It would cost $38,000.00. U.S. dollars for 10,000 copies! This delayed the printing another year.

COST MET

In October of 2002, I made another two month trip to Hong Kong. Vern and I had just become engaged through a telephone romance, sight unseen for over forty years. Vern was in Denver and I was in Wisconsin. More details on this courtship will follow in another chapter. Here I just want to tie in the connection with the printing of the colloquial Mongolian New Testament. I had to keep our engagement secret until my trip was over. While in Hong Kong, I wanted to hear what God had been doing in the lives of my former seminary students. Once they'd heard of my upcoming wedding, that's all they'd want to talk about.

While in Hong Kong, I spoke in several churches there and made known the cost of printing this colloquial Mongolian New Testament. The Chinese churches gave around (U.S.) $12,000.00 toward its printing. When I returned to the United States in December 2002, I stopped off for 9 days in Denver to see Vern, to get approved by Covenant Village to become a resident, to participate in a wedding reception there and to meet Vern's family. I then flew to Minneapolis and caught a ride home to announce our engagement to my shocked family and church. For our 2003 Valentine wedding, we requested no wedding gifts because we were both downsizing. Our email announcement read, "If you want to do something to please us, write a check to our church for the printing of the Mongolian New Testament". To our amazement $24,860.00 came in as wedding gifts for this cause. Combined with the Hong Kong giving, that was enough for New Life Literature, Hong Kong, to print 10,000 copies! When we arrived at Covenant Retirement Village on Nov. 1, 2003, the first air-mailed copy was here waiting for us! What a wedding present!

DISTRIBUTION HANG-UP

For two years these testaments sat in boxes in Hong Kong, unable to reach the Mongols. The difficulty was how to get these 10,000 testaments into Inner Mongolia. The German Mongol Mission that we had counted on for distribution had to leave Mongolia due to a moral problem. We lacked contacts with the nomadic Mongols scattered across the pasture lands of Inner Mongolia. I still had contacts with Chinese Christians who had known my father but the Chinese were very afraid to receive the boxes of New Testaments by either train or truck and then store or distribute them. Under a Communist government, this was risky business. How and where could they be safely stored? How could the Chinese Christians discreetly deliver them to the scattered Mongols?

After I shared this roadblock at a Covenant Retirement Village Vesper Service, the Lord specially laid this problem on the hearts of two lady residents. They prayed daily, incessantly, for these testaments to reach the Mongols. After many months of prayer, God used an American retired school teacher to answer those prayers. He went to Inner Mongolia to distribute Chinese-English bi-lingual New Testaments in the cities there that were heavily populated with Chinese. He found, for example, a Chinese church of several thousand. A converted Mongolian lady was interpreting the Chinese pastor's sermons from Chinese to Mongolian. The result was a thousand Christian Mongols in that congregation even though they had no

Bible that they could read. When this American teacher heard of the ten thousand Mongolian testaments available at New Life Literature, Hong Kong, he became our contact person to distribute them to other Mongols by hiring teams of Christian and non-Christian Mongols to accomplish this.

ANOTHER STRAND

Eventually we heard that the New Testaments had been well received and there were requests for thousands more. Providentially, one copy fell into the hands of a Mongolian publisher within Inner Mongolia. When he read through this whole New Testament in his heart language, he believed and offered to reprint it locally in quantity at a much reduced cost using cheaper paper. Funds were generously donated from the United States in response to one email request so thousands more have since been printed in country and distributed. A few thousand copies also included Genesis and Psalms. (That is all of the Old Testament that had been translated into Mongolian.) Because it takes four times the space to write in Mongolian script than in English and this was not India paper, these copies were too huge and heavy to be practical. In addition to thousands of copies of the whole New Testament, we funded the printing in-country of many more copies of just Luke /John: Luke for the life of Christ and John His teachings. These portions would include enough Gospel to lead a Mongol to Christ and be convenient to carry. The in-country publisher was eventually caught so he had to quit publishing these, and at least one distributor that I know of was imprisoned for a time. Still the Gospel has been spread and many Mongols now have received the printed Word. FEBC beams daily short wave Mongolian broadcasts into Inner Mongolia. One Mongolian convert who is a medical school graduate is now producing these daily broadcasts for FEBC to reach his own people.

Thank God for the internet. This is another thread. The German Mongol Mission put the entire Mongolian colloquial New Testament plus Genesis and Psalms on the web so it is available for all Mongols around the world who have computers to read. Within the first two years, the site already received 250,000 hits! You can see it yourself at the following web address: www.mongolbible.com .

TAPESTRY REVEALED

When looking back on so many seemingly insignificant and miscellaneous incidents, we begin to see God's handiwork--the many, colorful threads that He was weaving into a remarkably beautiful tapestry for His glory, all orchestrated to give the whole New Testament to one unreached people group in a script and version that they could read and understand! May God be praised!

Chapter 9

AVAILABLE UNTO DEATH

In 1934 John and Betty Stam were new young missionaries serving in South China under the China Inland Mission (CIM). Communist guerillas were active across China sporadically targeting foreigners and missionaries. John's letter below was his last. It gives a glimpse into the Stams' crisis and their feelings. (Our family was in North China at that time. Although my parents were aware of the dangers, they continued their ministry undaunted while shielding us children from fear.)

JOHN'S LETTER

Dear Brethren:
My wife, baby and myself are today in the hands of the
Communists in the city of Tsingteh. Their demand is
twenty thousand dollars for our release.
All our possessions and stores are in their hands, but
we praise God for peace in our hearts and a meal
tonight. God grant you wisdom in what you do, and us
fortitude, courage and peace of heart. He is able—and
a wonderful Friend in such a time.
Things happened so quickly this a.m. They were in the
city just a few hours after the ever-persistent rumors

really became alarming, so that we could not prepare to leave in time. We were just too late.
The Lord bless and guide you, and as for us, may God be glorified whether by life or by death.

In Him,

John C. Stam

INTO GOD'S HANDS

The next day after this letter, they were marched through the city, humiliated and only partially dressed; then the couple was forced to kneel where they committed their lives into God's hands. With large machetes, the Communists chopped off first John's head and then Betty's.

After the guerillas had left, Chinese Christians came out of hiding and found the Stam's three month old baby girl wrapped in blankets with two five dollar bills lovingly pinned inside the blankets. This money helped them to find a Chinese nursing mother to feed her and later to smuggle her to her maternal grandparents, Dr. and Mrs. Scott who were also missionaries in another part of China and finally to America where her aunt raised her. As demonstrated in the Stams' lives, being available to God can be costly!

The Chinese Christians tenderly dressed John and Betty and moved their bodies and heads down to the missionary cemetery in the city of Wu Hu where they were given a martyr's burial.

THE STAM FAMILY

The martyred John Stam was one of seven brothers who were leaders in various Christian ministries across America. John and Betty's martyrdom was a tragedy making national headline news that shocked America. A moving book, THE TRIUMPH OF JOHN AND BETTY STAM, was published about the lives and martyrdom of these two gifted and dedicated missionaries.

The John Stam that my Wheaton roommate, Doris, married was six years old when his uncle John was martyred, deeply impressing the young John to eventually become a missionary himself in Costa Rica. In fact many of the extended Stam family were challenged by the martyrdom to serve God in the far-flung mission fields of Africa, India, Ecuador, Alaska, Italy, France, and the United States ministries such as Young Life. Surely, John and Betty's lives were not wasted by their death.

My roommate, Doris, and husband, John, had long wanted me to travel with them into China to try to locate the graves of their martyred relatives. They hoped that with my knowledge of the language I could be their guide. By using the book "THE TRIUMPH OF JOHN AND BETTY STAM", they hoped we could discover clues to find their graves.

AVAILABLE TO TRAVEL

Due to my teaching schedule, I was not available for this until the end of May in 1997, when I retired from our mission, having served that last year on home assignment in the United States. Anyway, I wanted to return to Hong Kong for the historic return of the colony from British hands to China. I was now free to join the Stams in this intriguing search. The Communist government had destroyed all cemeteries in China some fifty years before this, so our search was a dubious adventure at best.

Since John could not clear his schedule when I was finally available, only his wife, Doris, and daughter, Becky, flew to Hong Kong to meet me there. They arrived the day AFTER the handover to China. Finally, the airlines that had been packed with thousands of reporters from around the world had empty seats available for them.

After booking a room for one night at the Shanghai YMCA through the Hong Kong YMCA, we boarded a beautiful new train from Hong Kong to Shanghai. We prayed for God's guidance on this humanly impossible mission.

During our many hours on this train, we interacted with many other passengers who were curious why these three Westerners on their train were heading for Wu Hu. One of these passengers, a Mr. Chan, was English speaking, very friendly and helpful.

He claimed to be a Seventh Day Adventist Christian (although he enjoyed his share of booze on that train). He said, "My brother is the organist at the large government registered church in Wu Hu!" What a coincidence! This Mr. Chan promised to phone his brother to expect us and be our guide in Wu Hu! Out of the one billion people in China, God surely had led us to this man on this train!

While we were booked that night at the Shanghai YMCA, Mr. Chan was going on to his home in Nanking which was our next stop after Shanghai. Mr. Chan arranged for us to meet him the next day in Nanking at the end of the #13 bus route coming from the train station. There he would wait for us and put us up for the night in his fitness center as his blessing on our way to Wu Hu. The three of us gals slept that night on soft exercise mats on the mezzanine floor of his fitness center! Again, God's incredible guidance and provision!

For night security, Mr. Chan locked us in with his roll-down steel door that was padlocked to the sidewalk hook below. "What if there's a fire?" I asked as we'd be locked in. "There won't be," he replied. At about midnight, a shower of rocks began hitting that steel roll-down door. The racket it made in the dead silence of night was terrifying. Fortunately for them, my two exhausted roommates slept through it all. I peeked out through our window between the multiple advertisement signs that extended over the sidewalk. These weren't young teens stoning us. They were full grown men! Had they seen us Western ladies enter that facility and not exit? Did they intend to smash their way in? These were frightening thoughts to identify with John and Betty Stam's possible feelings sixty-three years before. After an hour the stoning abruptly stopped and the steel roll-down door that protected both glass door and shop display window had held. Thank God for protection; but sleep did not come quickly.

In the morning, Mr. Chan came on a bike with steamed buns from the market for our breakfast. He unlocked the roll-down steel door to open his shop and let us out; then he saw us to our train station for a long train ride to Wu Hu.

Upon reaching Wu Hu by mid-morning, we tried several taxis before finding one whose driver knew the location of the large registered government approved church. We wanted to find the pastor and the organist, Mr. Chan, to see if anyone knew the location of the former missionary cemetery. That is where our book on the life of John and Betty Stam stated that they were buried. The church caretakers and cleaning personnel told us that all the church staff was out in the villages ministering during the week. This was Thursday. We must return Sunday morning if we wanted to meet any pastors.

THE YELLOW MOUNTAINS

My companions had the "Lonely Planet" travelers' handbook on China which showed us how to make good use of the several intervening days until

Sunday. The Yellow Mountains of China are famous for their incredible beauty--a "must see" for China travelers. Five or six hours by train would bring us to the foot of the mountains by evening and on the next day cable cars could take us up the mountain.

Little did we realize how difficult that train ride from Wu Hu to the mountain foothills would be! The train was crowded beyond belief. All seats were taken. The aisles were packed tight with people sitting on the floor or on their luggage. People were sitting on both the top of the little tables between facing seats as well as squatting UNDER those tables. Between the cars, people were dangerously hanging on as the train swung and lurched but at least they got air. We were soaked with sweat. We had to pull our suitcases that we packed for a month of travel. With arthritis in my legs and feet there was no way I could stand in the aisle on that moving train for the next six hours! It looked impossible to even get on board.

But God sent a soldier boy to help us. He was so polite and caring to us. He urged us to get on the train and push our way through that packed aisle. "Excuse us, please, excuse us, please" brought many dirty looks. Soldiers have much authority in China, so he kept commanding, "Please move, please move." At his command, the people who were filling the aisle between rows of seats squeezed together to let us and our luggage pass. The soldier insisted that we must work our way up to the fourth car which was the dining car where we could get seats. The last car before the dining car had one corner enclosed with iron bars for the conductor's protection. The soldier ordered the conductor to open the dining car for us. He obeyed! Once inside the dining car we had to order food which was very poor; but we were grateful to have seats for the rest of that ride, thanks to the soldier boy. Maybe he was an angel.

It was dark when we reached the mountain foothills where most passengers disembarked. It would have been extremely difficult in the dark in a strange town and among so many travelers searching for a room to find a place for us that night. The soldier told us to wait in the station while he went into the town to find an inn for us which he did. As foreigners, our room would have cost much more if we had booked it ourselves. Nor would we likely have found one ourselves. Before leaving, our soldier-guide instructed us how to locate the cable car for the mountains the next morning. In looking back, to get this kind of guidance seems almost miraculous. We experienced God's promise, "I will guide thee with mine eye."

The next morning a string of full cable cars took us across a beautiful forested valley to the top of the mountain range to a spectacular view. We were told that on only about three days a year is that mountain clear of clouds for such a view where we could see all over. God blessed us with one of those clear days.

After a lot of hiking, feasting at a mountain top restaurant and a cable car ride back down, that Friday flew by. After another night in a primitive inn, we visited some hot springs and toured the town Saturday morning. In the afternoon we headed for the train station. A group of delightful college students who had visited the Yellow Mountains and were on their way back north to school were walking with us toward the train station. They were eager to practice their English on real foreigners! The young fellows were so courteous and helpful. They tossed our heavy suitcases on their shoulders like they were nothing. This was a great blessing for we had to climb one flight of stairs to get over one train and down the next flight to climb stairs again over the next train several times until we got to our train. They were taking our same train but were heading farther north than us. Thankfully, this returning train was not so crowded. We had a lot of fun with those students so the ride seemed much shorter.

We had opportunity to share the Gospel with them which they had never heard before. They listened intently. They asked us where we were headed. When we replied "Wu Hu," they exclaimed, "Oh, thief city!" Apparently, Wu Hu was notorious for its breakdown of law and order. "What time will you arrive there?" When we answered "12:15 midnight," they groaned aloud in horror. We planned to stay in the train station dormitory. Every train station in China had one.

We three gals were the only ones to get off the train there. I asked two cleaning women in the station, the only people there at that time of night, for the location of the train dormitory. They waved toward the station exit and said "Outside, outside." Looking outside, we saw a half circle of shops, all with steel roll-down doors protecting their front. There were no street lights. Up ahead there seemed to be an island of buildings with some lights in the center of a wide road. What could we do?

THE BIKE LADY

As we stood in the dark wondering, a Chinese woman rode up to us on her bike. Dropping her bike, she asked us in Mandarin what do we need? "The train dormitory." "Oh, this way," she said. Leaving her bike, she grabbed my suitcase by the handle and dashed off, pulling it and leaving me far behind. Doris and Becky were pulling their suitcases and straining to keep up. I feared my luggage would disappear. The night was sticky hot. We were wet with sweat. We thought this woman was recruiting business for her train dormitory. She soon came back with my suitcase, herself wet with sweat, saying that the entrance to the train hotel was not on that side of the island. "Let's try the other side," she suggested. Obviously she was NOT recruiting guests for the hotel since she didn't even know where the entrance was.

This time we found the hotel entrance and the four of us stepped inside to verify that it was the hotel and to book our room. When I turned to our bike-lady to offer her money for her help, she shook her head and refused it. I knew that in China, no one goes out of their way to help someone for nothing! I was taken back that she refused the money. Puzzled, I wondered, who she was and WHY had she helped us? So I asked, "Then WHY did you help us?" She mumbled an answer in Mandarin as the hotel clerk pressed to see my passport. I handed it over and turned back to talk further with the bike lady. She was gone and nowhere to be seen! She seemed to have just disappeared! I dashed for the door to look up and down the street. No one!

We were shown to our whitewashed room that was simply furnished with three cots plus mosquito netting for each. There was water for bathing and a single fluorescent light tube hung from the high ceiling.

Now we three travelers had time to think. We wondered, "Who was that bike lady?" How could she have just disappeared? Why did she put herself out to help us total strangers and then refuse a tip? I could only conclude, "She must have been an angel!" I could find no other explanation. We thanked the Lord together for an incredible night as we experienced God's care, guidance and protection at midnight in "thief city!"

FINDING THE CEMETERY

On Sunday morning we caught a cab to the government registered church. We did not know the time of the first service which was already in progress. What first met my eyes was the entire churchyard crowded with an outside audience of rows of people sitting side by side on five inch high stools but Doris' first impression was of the extremely long row of parked bicycles outside the church. Next was the crowded courtyard. This was the church's overflow crowd. Inside every seat was taken. What a picture of spiritual hunger!

I was embarrassed when the ushers cleared the front row for us, insisting that as guests we get an inside seat. I noticed the organist, no doubt the brother to the Mr. Chan who had hosted us in his Nanking fitness shop; so this Mr. Chan was expecting us. The pastor was preaching in an off-brand of Mandarin which I did not understand. When the service was over, I introduced us to Mr. Chan the organist. He spoke good English! Neither he nor the pastor had been there long or had any idea where the Stams were buried sixty-three years before.

I asked, "Is there anyone in your congregation who has been here long enough to know and remember where the old missionary cemetery was located?" "No, unless our 86 year-old evangelist. He is probably the only one still living who might remember the Stam martyrdom and know where they were buried; but he was not here today. We will try to contact him for you."

Eventually, they reached him by phone and found that he was ill, so he was unable to meet us. We decided to stay overnight to try again the next day. We even contacted the police to see if they had any record of where the old missionary cemetery had been. They had no idea. They said that all the cemeteries in China had been destroyed fifty some years ago, leaving no trace.

On Monday morning Mr. Chan, the organist, had contacted the evangelist by phone to find him well and happy to meet us. With organist Chan directing our taxi, we arrived near where the evangelist lived. There we ladies waited for Mr. Chan to locate the evangelist. Addresses in China are not so specific. He lives somewhere down the third lane after the railroad tracks! We three ladies waited while Mr. Chan searched and inquired down that lane until he located the delightful, lively elderly gentleman for us. We were invited into his simple room in the row of dwellings where he greeted us joyously, and spoke to us in good English. Incredibly, he not only knew the location of the old missionary cemetery, it was within walking distance of where we were. No need even for a taxi!

I discovered that these people were used to walking! Although our evangelist friend was 86, much older than us, still we could hardly keep up with him. To me it was a very long walk. Eventually we came to a large, beautiful, fenced-in grassy park-like area with uniformed police guarding the barred entrance gate. Our evangelist told us to hold back while he walked ahead to gain permission from the guard to let us in.

On one side of the beautifully mowed park was an impressive brick building which we were told was an elite fitness center for government people. We did not check that out.

A brook flowed through this lovely small enclosed park. The brook was spanned by an ornate bridge of old Chinese style. However, most signifcant to us was the lovely grove of yellow bamboo which graced one end of that park. Our evangelist friend told us that the old missionary cemetery was under that beautiful bamboo grove! He knew and remembered. He could testify that those missionary graves had never been disturbed. How ironic! Even the local government did not know that while all known cemetery land had long been redeveloped for more important use, yet the atheistic Communist government had, unknowingly, carefully preserved the remains of God's old warriors in this beautiful way! Doris and her daughter took many pictures. God's sense of humor! Had Chinese Christians decades ago planted this bamboo to hide and protect the graves of these beloved messengers from God? How marvelously God had led us in our search to find their graves, to a spot probably known only to God and to this very special aged evangelist!

We three ladies took Mr. Chan and the evangelist out for a good Chinese restaurant meal. The cost was very reasonable but the meal was a luxury to them. It was so special that both of these men spoke English so that we could fellowship, ask questions and visit in English. Doris gave the evangelist her English New Testament which he deeply treasured for he had none in English. I told Mr. Chan the organist that I had a bi-lingual Chinese-English New Testament in my suitcase that was checked in security back at the train station to give him. He too was delighted to get it. Back at the station the men pointed out a mural that was painted across the top of the train station wall which depicted the city of Wu Hu. Two hills were painted there with a valley in between. They pointed to that valley as the location of the old missionary cemetery. "If you ever return and want to find that old cemetery again, show your taxi driver that valley on the mural and he will take you there! Mission accomplished beyond what we had dared to hope!

Before boarding the train, we bid final farewell to these two precious brothers in Christ and gave thanks to God for helping us successfully find, not just a needle in a haystack but a single sacred graveyard in the vast land of China. Doris, Rebecca and I rode back by train to Shanghai where our ways parted. My travel companions flew back to North America and Costa Rica while I traveled north to Outer Mongolia by economy train to teach English at a basketball/English youth camp there. But that is another story.

MONGOLIAN YOUTH CAMPS

During the forty some years that the Soviet Union controlled Outer Mongolia, summer youth camps run by the government became the norm. The government used this means to identify budding leaders. These key youth then were honored by being sent off to Russia for training and indoctrination in Communism. After Russia pulled out of Mongolia in the early 1990's (it was too expensive to maintain, I was told), youth camps had become a summer tradition.

AN EFFECTIVE TOOL

Since basketball was a favorite sport among the Mongols and a nationally famous, exceptionally tall Mongolian basketball star had become a vibrant Christian, a door of opportunity was opened.

Christian missionaries together with Mongol Christians grasped this chance to sponsor a ten-day youth camp coaching teens in both basketball and English. The prospect of English teachers from America plus this star basketball player as coach made this particular camp especially inviting. Well over fifty kids enrolled, each coming with a roll of bedding and clothes, excitedly piling into one of several very old buses hired for the occasion. A distant summer camp site nestled at the edge of a forested hill was our destination. Just getting to the site was an adventure in itself with the crowded buses slowly bumping over the ruts that served as roads.

The camp boasted simple primitive cabins. With my own sleeping bag, I shared an especially nice cabin for teachers with a lovely bi-lingual Mongolian Christian lady whose fellowship I grew to treasure. She was helping to run our camp.

The campers ranged in age from twelve to upper teens. They ate in two shifts according to age, filling the dining hall twice at each meal. A water truck came each morning to supply just enough water for the kitchen, for drinking water and water for the campers to wash their faces and brush their teeth over open outdoor troughs.

They were delightful kids, happy, excited and eager to face each new day in these unfamiliar surroundings. They of course spoke Mongolian; but bi-lingual Mongol girls, in their late teens or early twenties, were our interpreters. About half of the campers signed up for basketball and the other half for English lessons. The English classes were divided into beginner, intermediate and advanced levels, with one or two American teachers plus interpreters for each level.

Our English teaching material, carefully prepared, published and bought from our Evangelical Free Church headquarters, entwined each English lesson with biblical material. For example, the days of the week were taught around the days of creation, the vocabulary involved with heavenly bodies, galaxies, and varieties of birds, fish, plants and animals. Foundational biblical truths were taught along with English.

On the last day of the camp, all participants were invited to attend a joint, final meeting in the largest open, covered meeting shelter. I was asked to give an evangelistic message through an interpreter. The influence of Russian Communism with its atheistic teaching was still deeply embedded in the worldview of the leaders in the new Mongolian government; so our missionaries working there at that time had to be quite guarded in what Christian doctrine they taught, especially to youth under eighteen. For example, one young boy of twelve from an elite English school asked me in perfect English, very seriously, and almost shocked, "Is it really true, did God REALLY create the world?" There would likely be flak to follow if he repeated my reply to his parents who were high up in government. Our team prayed much for the camp, especially for that final evangelistic meeting just before our leaving. I really poured my heart out to give them the Gospel of God's love that sent His Son to die for our sins. I remember some positive responses especially among the interpreters.

Our Mongolian missionaries encouraged me to present the Gospel clearly, fully, openly, although they could not do so if they wished to remain in Mongolia. They explained that I could do so because later when they'd get flak from the powers that be, they could always blame me: "Oh, that American teacher who spoke her religious teachings here so openly, she has long since left Mongolia!! " Since I was no longer around to be deported, the problem was solved! Outside speakers at the youth camp enjoyed more freedom in sowing the Gospel seed. Is that being "wise as serpents and harmless as doves"?

I never did find out whom to thank for their special consideration, effort and expense to make a Western-style toilet for us foreign teachers. Constructed as a single unit with men's and women's sides back to back, the inside finish was gleaming white tile. Western-style sinks and toilets completed a very impressive facility which one would hardly expect to find at a primitive camp in barren Mongolia! But there was just one problem. NO WATER! So the facility was never used. We still had to run into the nearby woods at the call of nature. A small inconvenience indeed for the privilege of sharing God's love with those precious kids!

From there (it was August 1997) I flew back to the comforts of the USA **<u>now available</u>** to begin my new retirement ministry among Chinese scholars at the University of Minnesota.

Chapter 10

COURTSHIP AND WEDDING

A tantalizing E-mail sent Dec. 15, 2002:

CHRISTMAS GREETINGS – A BLESSED FALL

*T*his special season we especially remember God's fantastic action TO PURSUE A LOVE RELATIONSHIP with us. He so loved the world that He sent His Son so whosoever believes in Him need not perish but have ETERNAL LIFE! And this life is in His Son. "He who HAS the Son HAS life and he who has Not the Son has not life." Wow!

On October 18th of this year (2002) I made another short-term missions trip to the Orient. Besides speaking in a number of Hong Kong churches (in Chinese) and connecting with old friends and former seminary students, my goal was to bring the Chinese, Mongols and Banjara Gypsies of India into that LOVE RELATIONSHIP; but God's ways sure ran counter to mine!

Upon arriving in Hong Kong I went first to our own Evangel Hospital to get my annual physical checkup. A week later when I returned to get my very excellent health report, I tripped in our own hospital falling so seriously that I became an INPATIENT for 5 days! I fell with that right leg that's been stiff so long from an old injury and it folded under me as I landed. My screams of pain brought immediate medical attention. This was NOT my plan. X-rays showed no broken bones but an MRI revealed a torn knee cartilage and torn ligament. For the rest of that two month mission's trip, I remained on crutches. The doctor said, "It's a miracle! People with a stiff leg like yours will go under full anesthesia to break loose that stiffness while you did it by accident! It will take a while but when that knee heals, you'll no longer have a stiff leg! It's a miracle!" (I'd rather have had anesthesia!)

UNEXPECTED VISITS

God had work for me in that hospital. He sent a patient in crisis with a very prepared heart to the bed next to mine. I had the great joy of guiding her into a LOVE RELATIONSHIP with God. "Lord, is that why I fell?"

Unfortunately, it's not always possible to staff a Christian hospital with all Christian nurses. God in His wisdom timed my stay there to lead two Evangel Hospital nurses, whose hearts He had prepared, into a personal relationship with Him while they were caring for me! Surely, my fall was in God's plan although not in mine. There were also many friends who I got to visit while in Evangel Hospital. Instead of me chasing around to find them, they came to the hospital to see me while I rested. It was a precious renewing of relationships!

And now to shorten this email, I'm skipping ahead to the END of my two-month missionary journey (which included escapades in both China and India). As to India, I'll just mention here my visit to the Banjara Gypsies of Hyderabad, India. They're a largely unreached people group with which I've long been involved. My home church in Wisconsin had given (U.S.) $3,000.00, enough for them to build a simple church building. On that visit while I was still on crutches, it was my joy to cut the ribbon for the dedication of that church building that was packed with 400 Gypsies sitting on the floor! Now, hopefully these Gypsies, too, can experience a Love Relationship with God!

AIRPORT DEPARTURE

Now in December and still lame, I needed help to get myself and my luggage to Hong Kong's massive new International Airport for my return to the United States. A former Evangel Seminary colleague offered to transport me in her van. She recruited Victor, one of her husband's University students, to help with my luggage. "NO," was his answer on the long drive to the airport. He was not a Christian. I shared with him a bit about Jesus. To express my appreciation for all their kindness, the trip to the airport, getting me a wheel chair and check in, I treated them to breakfast in the airport. *In a casual conversation over noodles, Victor revealed, "I need a belief system for my life. I don't know which way is right. I'm praying to Buddha now but my life is so empty." (These pagan religions have no concept of a God like ours who LOVES us.) So I asked Victor, "Do you think you'd like SOMEDAY to experience a love relationship with this Creator God we've been talking about?" Slowly he nodded. I asked him, "When would be a good time to begin? Next year?"*

I waited and prayed through a long silence. "NOW "was his surprising response! What rejoicing as, shortly before takeoff on my homeward flight, we saw the joy on Victor's face as HE began HIS LOVE RELATIONSHIP with our God!

CLIFF HANGER

My further exploits and adventures with God in China (regarding the Mongolian New Testament and shortwave Mongolian Gospel broadcasts) and in the Gypsy villages of India must wait until a later email to relate or this would get too lengthy; but first, here's a peek into another INCREDIBLE STORY of a LOVE RELATIONSHIP that I experienced on this trip.!!!!!!!!!!!!!!!!!!!!!!!!!!!!!!!!!!!!

Topping off all these blessings on my Orient mission's trip was my 9-day stop-over in Denver, Colorado, which culminated in a DIAMOND RING FOR ME! A Valentine Wedding to follow next February 15th in my Wisconsin home church!! Details of THIS

LOVE RELATIONSHIP will follow shortly in the next email!

(The following email crisscrossed the world!)

MY PERSONAL LOVE STORY

To top off the blessings of this Orient missions trip was a 9-day stop-over in Denver, Colorado that culminated in a diamond ring for me!!! The roots of this incredible story date back four decades.

As a missionary on home assignment in 1957, I was sent to Sioux Falls, South Dakota to speak at an EFC mission conference. After locating the church I went there to seek directions to the parsonage where I was to have supper and spend the night. Only a soot-covered workman was there fixing the church furnace. When he directed me to the parsonage next door, I asked "And who might you be?" He replied, "Oh, I'm the janitor here." That evening when the pastor joined the family for supper, I was surprised to see that janitor WAS Pastor Vern Olson —a "fix anything kind of guy"! After speaking that night in his church, I went my way. When we crossed paths once later at an EFC National Conference, we laughed when I addressed him as "The Janitor!"

*This summer of 2002 and forty-five years later, I got a surprising phone call. "**This is the janitor calling!**" I had lost track of him for decades; but this time he wasn't laughing. He was devastated and overwhelmed with loneliness, having lost his beloved* *wife the past winter. He'd been looking through the EFC mission's prayer guide, which he used faithfully, for old friends in ministry with whom to share his grief and loneliness. When he phoned his old Trinity school-mate, Roger Anderson, he found the Andersons were struggling with severe medical challenges. "They've got enough problems" he concluded. He asked Roger about me as someone in that prayer guide to unload on because the Andersons and I had been colleagues for years in Hong Kong. Upon the Anderson's recommendation, Vern phoned me to unload on.*

I sympathized as I remembered my dad's loneliness in the same situation. I prayed with him over the phone and said, if he needed a shoulder to cry on, I'd be available; "BUT I must make it clear up front, I'm NOT interested in marriage!" "I'm not either," he said, still grieving.

Daily phone calls continued. The more I came to know this transparent, Godly man from the hours on the phone, the more I admired his qualities. It was uncanny how much common ground we shared: same life goals, life direction, values, standards, life patterns and habits, the same Swedish heritage and Evangelical Free Church denomination. We both grew up under the influence of a daily family altar, as well as dairy farm experience—me in Wisconsin, he in Nebraska. We'd attended the same schools and knew the same people. He was on the Trinity Divinity School faculty when I was a student there but our paths always just missed. Personal evangelism and church planting were his passion as well as mine. God had used him to organize 42 new Evangelical Free Churches which included the Deerfield, Illinois EFC while he was teaching at Trinity! I soon discovered that this former farm boy, besides pastoring and organizing new churches, had taught in four colleges and four seminaries around the world!

As a young missionary, I had told God that I wished to serve Him with all the strength and energy of my youth, unencumbered with family. I could marry after retirement, not before; but retirement blessings and Chinese ministry brought such contentment and I so valued my independence that I was no longer interested. I'd dismissed marriage opportunities after retirement and I planned to stay put where I was until death.

When Dr. Vern Olson asked early on if he could eventually meet me when he would come to the October missions celebration at Crystal Free Church in Minneapolis, I consented because my life wasn't mine to control; but I emphasized that I was so content where I was, "even God could hardly move me. He'd have to do something pretty drastic to move me away from here before I die!" Here in Wisconsin I have family, my home church and friends, a Chinese ministry in the Twin Cities, a big garden and I was renting a lovely, hundred-year-old farm-house that was in an ideal setting in the country above the bubbling Trade River below.

Furthermore, I thought my life had been so unique that there'd be no man alive who could really understand or relate to where I'd been most of my life in the Orient. After growing up on our Wisconsin farm, I'd had forty-four years in Hong Kong doing student work, literature distribution, church planting, personal evangelism and the last thirty-five years teaching in Evangel Seminary.

When I learned that, besides being involved in similar ministries, one of those seminaries where Vern had taught was in my Evangel Seminary in Hong Kong, it blew my mind! Unknown to me, he had come as a short-term teacher to Evangel Seminary in 1996 just after I left Evangel for arthritis treatment and Mandarin study in China! Having taught my Chinese students in my school, he would know and understand first hand of my last thirty-five years of ministry there! Could all this be just coincidence? It looked more and more like a "God thing." If God had really engineered all these circumstances, I couldn't wiggle out of this relationship so easily. I pushed these thoughts aside because I was unwilling to face them. Neither did I dare to discourage his phone calls which had grown to an hour or more each morning and evening! After so many hours of phone calls for days, weeks and months, we'd really come to know and understand each other inwardly. I counted this as a "ministry" to help one of God's old warriors! To him it grew to mean much more.

When Vern proposed to me over the phone, (we still hadn't seen each other for over 40 years!) I told him that I respected him and admired all that I knew of him but I wasn't emotionally involved; "but I know some missionary gals who really WANT to get married. Let me introduce you to some of them." I'll never forget his reply. "No, I want YOU and I'll wait for you as long as it takes!" Eventually he won! I couldn't ignore the mounting evidence that God was bringing us together. I became convinced this would be an "arranged marriage"--arranged by God!

It was uncanny how telemarketers cooperated. "Our company will offer you 200 free domestic long distance minutes if you'll try our phone service." Just when they were used up, another company offered 1000 free domestic minutes. Right when those expired and my last month before this trip, we were offered ONE MONTH of unlimited free domestic phone calls! How well we used them!

Vern and I were pledged to each other by phone before my Orient trip. Yet, if I wanted to see my former students in Hong Kong and to hear what God was doing in THEIR lives, I must keep these plans secret. If they knew that I was soon to marry, that's all they'd want to talk about! So we kept our plans secret. Aside from my pastor and his wife, no one else had an inkling! On my way home from this Orient missions trip, I could spend nine days in Denver with Vern and his family. There an official engagement presented with a diamond ring, accepted as a Covenant Retirement Village resident, and then home to share the news for the first time with my family and home church! Finally, one email and all Hong Kong would know our NEWS OF THE CENTURY! Such was our plan.

There are a good 8,000 Chinese in the metro Denver area. Pastor Vern Olson was instrumental in starting the Chinese Free Church of Denver which is now pastored by a couple of my former Evangel Seminary students. What an opportunity to minister together among the Denver Chinese as a TEAM as God opens doors!

We plan a February 15th Valentine wedding at 2:00 p.m. in the Trade River Evangelical Free Church, about 1 ½ hours North of St. Paul. Then, after the honeymoon and sufficient time to dispose of my extra stuff in Wisconsin (we're putting 2 households together into a tiny condo so we don't need any wedding gifts), we will settle in a one-bedroom condo in Covenant Retirement Village (located in Westminster, a northwest suburb of Denver). With some insurance money that Vern got for a serious, rear-ended car accident Vern had, (requiring six back surgeries) and pooling our resources, we decided to buy into this Covenant Village where I will join Vern next year. An additional hefty monthly fee covers electricity, heat, air conditioning, cable TV, linens, laundry, etc., plus a daily dress-up dinner that compares to a Hilton Hotel! After such simple living in Hong Kong, I may even feel uncomfortable living there in such luxury! With our combined social security and pensions we should just make it financially.

To us a major attraction there is the guaranteed care until death, even when your money runs out! We will not need to burden others as we age. Besides the independent condo living, assisted living is provided when needed and finally, full medical care, including assisted living, skilled nursing and Alzheimer's care. It suits me fine that Denver has especially low humidity!

The view from our condo picture window is of the snow-capped Rocky Mountains. One floor below us is an indoor swimming pool with hot tub, sauna and a fully equipped fitness center, not to mention the excellent pastor's library, a wood-working shop and craft center. There's even a small plot for gardening. The whole complex covers 27 manicured acres. Most of Vern's family lives in the immediate vicinity. Surely we are abundantly blessed!

It seems my whole life has been a series of miracles. This new move is frosting on the cake. Little did I realize when I chose to give God my best years that he would reward me with a retirement beyond my wildest dreams— including a wonderful, Godly husband that I hadn't even prayed for. While I had the joy of serving Him in Hong Kong, someone else was going through labor pains and giving me a ready-made family of five children and eighteen grandchildren, all of whom love the Lord! I anticipate growing to know them. I'm overwhelmed with blessings. As Hebrews 11:6 states, "Surely, GOD IS A REWARDER of those who diligently seek Him".

Doris Ekblad
Vernon & Doris Ekblad-Olson
Doris.EkbladOlson@gmail.com

INSIGHTS FROM THIS EXPERIENCE

Shortly before our wedding, I shared our love story with about a hundred Chinese scholars at the University of Minnesota friendship dinner. I used our story to make the following evangelistic application:

It occurred to me, that while Vern was pursuing a love relationship with me, God is pursuing a love relationship with you. There's no other religion that has a God who loves you. Their gods are to be feared. Our "*God so loved the world*" that He gave His only Son that we might come into a love relationship with Him. It is sin that has separated us from God. That's why God seems so far away. It was sin that came in and marred our earth, brought suffering, fighting, hurt, discord and loneliness because we're separated from God. If sin could get into heaven, it would spoil heaven too. We all have sin; and I can't help you because the wages of sin is death and I've got sin. I can't care for my own sin. Because Jesus had no sin and because He was God, His death could cover the sins of the whole world. God made that sacrifice in sending His own son. Because He so loves us, He wants to pursue a love relationship with us.

You know, God is saying "I love you and I'll wait for you as long as it takes." He won't force you.

Maybe you have experienced a one-sided love and you know how much it hurts. That's how God feels when you refuse His love. I find that responding to Vern gives me many other blessings; but you know, responding to God will give you far more.

In the garden of Eden Adam and Eve listened to Satan's lie. His lie was this: They were forbidden to eat of the fruit of one tree as a test of their obedience. Satan said to them, "If you eat of that tree, you'll have the knowledge of good and evil. You will become as God." They wanted to become their own god and that has been Satan's trick ever since. "If you believe in Jesus, you'll lose your independence." Do you realize that instead God will set us free from those habits and things that bind us? You will be free to enjoy all the bountiful blessings that God has prepared.

My advice to you is: don't make the mistake I almost made and refuse something very wonderful. God wants a personal relationship with you. Those of us who have experienced that relationship, like those of you who are married and have a good marriage, will realize how foolish my original response was. Those of us who have experienced that relationship with God wish so much that you could experience it too. We can't fully describe it. You have to experience it yourself. The Bible uses the marriage relationship as an illustration of the relationship that God wants to have with us. Marriage in its ideal form is the closest thing on earth to that. God is offering this to you today.

Respond to Him by saying, "Lord, forgive me for clinging to my independence. Thank you for sending Jesus to die on the cross and to pay for my sin. I know that I can't get into heaven with sin, but the blood of Jesus will wash away my sin. I trust You today. I submit to You as my Lord." Then, you can enter into a love relationship that's far greater than what I can have with Vern. Whenever you think of our wedding, remember that God is pursuing a love relationship with you. You can begin it today in your own heart by that response to Him.

Vern and Doris Ekblad-Olson

Chapter 11

TRAVELING TOGETHER

OUR GOAL

In March, 2005, Vern and I joined six leaders of the Denver Chinese Evangelical Free Church for a two week mission trip to Panama. Our team included four laymen plus the pastor and his wife who were both my former students and graduates of Evangel Seminary, Hong Kong. We hoped to help and encourage Pastor Samuel Wai, who was planting a Chinese Evangelical Free Church in Panama City. I had been to Panama before, and been impressed by not only the fascinating Panama Canal but also by the huge Chinese population and cemetery there, compared to the small Chinese Gospel witness! My concern was where had those Chinese gone for eternity.

OUR METHOD

In order to build contacts with the locals, Vern and I were scheduled to teach English while others of our team would teach computer science. For this our team brought extra computers along. We were surprised upon arrival to find that there had been no pre-registration of students or information on how many students to expect or on their English or computer levels. Apparently, in the culture there, things were done more "spontaneously". We needed to accept their culture and build relationships. While teaching English, we planned to weave in the Gospel story. Among other activities, I was scheduled to bring the morning message one Sunday in Cantonese and Vern the next Sunday through an interpreter.

POWER SECRET

This church plant had started from scratch two years previously, and now it had a small congregation of around 40. We prayed to be led to prepared hearts and for solid spiritual fruit from our contacts. We knew that a spiritual harvest would depend on prayer; so I recruited a team of faithful email prayer partners to stand with us, sharing God's heart for those "displaced Chinese" in Panama City. My most important contribution on the team would be my connecting with those prayer partners and keeping them updated by email. Obviously, just the eight of us in two weeks could accomplish little for eternity; but an enlarged team of prayer warriors from both the United States and Hong Kong, kept in close prayer touch by email, could make a huge difference! We set out with anticipation to storm the Enemy's strongholds!

Our team spent every forenoon together in prayer and sharing. We knew that's where our strength lay although we had no idea of the tangled, messed up lives we would encounter. For most of our team, this

was their first mission trip experience. We also hoped to
bring back to the whole Denver Chinese Free Church
a burden and vision for missions. So much was at stake.

OUR WEAKNESS

Early on we sensed the Enemy's opposition
to Vern and me going. I'd had a couple of heart
procedures a month before. Both Vern and I had just
recovered from a viral upper respiratory flu. All the
more we wanted to be available to actively serve our
Lord while we still could. We did get medical clearance
from our doctor for the trip. Unfortunately, the doctor
gave me pills that wiped out my sleep for three straight
nights (as well as my immune system) just before our
trip, which eventually landed me in a Panama hospital!
Vern lost his balance a few hours before our flight,
falling backwards and hitting his back on a corner table.
Excruciating pain followed which added to that from his
previous back problems. Had he injured his spleen or a
kidney? In that last minute it was either a trip to the
emergency room of a hospital or on to Panama! Vern
chose to go to Panama. He would manage by taking
pain pills and a cane.

OUR QUARTERS

In the house rented for our team's stay, wall air-
conditioners in the bedrooms brought welcome
nighttime relief from the heat and humidity; but our
beds were just mattresses on the floor. They were very

comfortable to sleep on once we got down there, but getting up and down at our age was a major challenge.

BEGINNING MINISTRY

The first evening, our team took part in the regular Friday fellowship meeting. The food and fellowship were drawing cards. One sister would prepare a Chinese meal to be followed by singing and a Gospel message.

In the car on the way to the service, I was asked to be the evening speaker! I asked "For how long?" "Oh, about an hour and a half!" was the reply. I was glad to share the speaking time with Vern, who spoke through a Chinese interpreter! We were caught off guard by such a laid back approach; yet, we sensed God speaking through us as we relied on Him. We knew our friends back home were praying. Around thirty came that evening. We all mingled , fellowshipped and got acquainted as we waited a full hour for that Chinese meal. Most of those attending were young people. Not all were Christians. Although I chaffed at the long wait, it turned out to be time well spent. Those Chinese people were out of their own environment, "displaced people," with complex social and family problems. For example, a young Christian fellow that Vern counseled had quit his job 3 months before, wanting to go to Bible school to train to serve the Lord and hoping someone would support him! His wife was not in agreement to this; so their marriage was in crisis. Just a sample of many problems we would soon encounter.

TANGLED LIVES

During one afternoon visitation, I met one young mother who had come to Christ through the loss of her husband to cancer two years before. As a single mom, she struggled to support her two daughters by working in a beauty salon. Her only pay was half of what her efforts brought in and business was slow. So two of us team mates went to give her some business--$6.00 U.S dollars for a haircut, ($3.00 to her)! She shared that one of her daughters, just 8 years old, had a rare blood disease so she needed a blood transfusion every month to stay alive! What pressures and heartaches! This was true of many Chinese we met there. Life was hard.

The owner or boss of the salon where that mother worked had his problems. I visited and prayed with him that afternoon. His heart was tender. He claimed to want to be a Christian and said he even prayed once to receive Christ. However, he felt he couldn't attend church because of the shady businesses he was involved in—a massage parlor to give work to single moms who'd been abandoned by their husbands but still had children to feed and support. Prostitution was also involved. The women were allowed to keep half of what they brought in to feed their children. He claimed to want to be helping them for that was all the work they could find! This boss said he had been trying for a whole year to sell the business in order to pay off his mortgage on the place! He felt his reputation was too bad to come to church until he could get rid of this bad business. The Chinese community there knew his connections and he said, "My coming to church would hurt the reputation of the church. I will come to church and make known my desire to follow Jesus when I can get rid of this business." Even worse, his Chinese wife didn't like Panama so she had divorced him and returned to China. If he'd really become a Christian, what should he do about the Panamanian woman he'd been living with, had a child by, and was partner with him in the salon business? Sin weaves a tangled web but Jesus CAME to set captives FREE! We longed to see the Gospel transform and untangle those tragic lives.

LAW AND ORDER PROBLEMS

Unemployment was high so there was much thieving and robberies. Chinese businesses were targeted the most because the Chinese were hard working, thrifty and saved their money. We were told that if a Panamanian worker was given a raise, he might stay home until he'd used up the extra money! So robbers would rather target the Chinese restaurants, homes and businesses.

A young Chinese mother came to church with her lower face covered. Robbers had burst into her shop for money. Although she held a baby in her arms, the robbers shot away her lower jaw with a rifle so she couldn't call the police! Now 7 years and 19 surgeries later, she still didn't want to show what remained of her face; but through this tragedy and the love showered on her by Chinese Christians, she had come to know and trust in Jesus.

OUR SCHEDULED CLASSES

There was considerable interest in the computer courses offered. About six students came to the classes with others coming for individual help. I'd have to rate our English course almost a disaster! Attendance was so erratic that you couldn't build language but we did build relationships.

SPIRITUAL WARFARE

Thanks to the faithful prayer backing, within the first four days, our team was led to eight Chinese with seeking, prepared hearts who were ready to receive Christ as Saviour! We also saw evidence of the Enemy fighting back. He attacked where it would hurt most-- our connection with our prayer partners.

I had a select list compiled on my desktop computer of prayer partners who were committed to pray for our Panama mission. Upon arriving in Panama, I discovered that those precious email addresses had failed to transfer to my laptop! They were the underpinning of our mission. To reconstruct a new select list of prayer partners by memory from the old outdated email addresses on my laptop was a huge task. Thank God, a solid prayer team did emerge which brought results.

The Enemy also used my missed sleep just before our trip to revive my viral flu and asthma, turning it into full blown bronchial viral pneumonia! Not what you'd wish for on a mission trip, but those few days in a top-notch Panama hospital gave me time to pray and daily connect with email partners as I shared our team's adventures and needs and generated a prayer covering. That was to be my main contribution to the mission anyway.

ASTHMA, A BLESSING

In 2003, I had been in Los Angeles speaking at a Chinese conference after which the Los Angeles fires surrounded the city with all exit roads closed. After inhaling smoke and ash for several days, I developed asthma. Although I never had an asthma attack, I had wheezed every night thereafter and was under continual treatment at the National Jewish Hospital in Denver, which is world famous for treating lung problems. We expected no cure, just treatments to control it; but in that Panama hospital, I was assigned an exceptionally brilliant and caring lung specialist who treated me intensively with both traditional and non-traditional medicine. In just five days of treatment, my symptoms were nearly gone. Just three days after walking out of that hospital, I was able to bring the Sunday morning message to the congregation. All God's grace! I have not wheezed at night since! No more need of treatment at National Jewish Hospital! My asthma problem was apparently gone because I was available for that Panama mission trip. What an unexpected blessing! Our travel insurance covered all medical expenses!

INTRODUCING PASTOR SAMUEL WAI

Samuel Wai, the local pastor, had taken early retirement from engineering to get re-treaded for ministry. He and his wife, Betty, in their 50's, offered themselves available to God for church planting among the Chinese in Panama City. Being very laid back, they were a perfect fit for that culture, with their relaxed, loving, winsome spirit, to reach out to the Chinese there! We needed to learn from them. Samuel and Betty were natural surrogate parents to so many displaced young people who were without family, and they drew them to Jesus like magnets. They both did much one-on-one evangelism and discipling since many Chinese who were running 'convenience stores' were not free to attend church. This made the ministry very labor intensive; but it surely paid off. I was impressed by the spiritual maturity of their new believers which was a result of this personal follow up. I wouldn't have expected such a worshipful spirit as was evident in the Sunday services from such new believers who were all less than two years old in the Lord.

TEAM STRATEGY

Our team members were mature, eager, full of energy, with a burden for souls and eager to introduce other Chinese to Jesus! They ran circles around Vern and me and were an inspiration to watch! Empowered from our forenoon group prayer and sharing times, they went forth in different directions to witness in tea-houses, shops and on the street. Some testified in a

Chinese school. Many Chinese convenience stores were a wide open door. Because business was slow, the clerks were bored and happy to have someone come in to talk with them which resulted in several decisions for Christ. Others were interviewed on the radio, for the church was buying time to run a 3-hour daily Chinese broadcast. This was very popular among the Chinese who were drawn by their own music and language.

Attendance on our second Sunday swelled to 60 people with another four individuals trusting Jesus that day. We saw the fruit of our team's unique approaches to reaching people for Christ as well as from our faithful prayer partners.

OUTREACH TO YOUTH

The team members creatively conveyed Biblical truth and values to over 50 Chinese youth on the two Sunday afternoons by competitions, drama and role-playing of Bible character. The team had prepared themselves beforehand so the Biblical stories and applications really came to life in a culturally relative way. The youth, many non-Christians, were so intent and involved in the Word presented this way that one team member commented, "I can't believe it. They didn't even take a bathroom break for 2 ½ hours!"

DINNER WITNESS

Following our first Sunday afternoon service, when the youth group finally wound down, we were invited to a lovely home for a late Chinese dinner served buffet style. (Family dinner there was often eaten after ten p.m.!) Our hostess was a new Christian of less than a year. Her husband attended services regularly and she was sure he believed; but in their living room was the old ancestor-worship material and idol shelf that he couldn't part with.

As we shook hands for good-by at the door, I asked him, "What is holding you back from following Jesus?" "Oh, I do believe," he confessed before all the guests. I pointed to the idol shelf, and he hastened to explain, "Oh, I haven't touched that even once this year!" I said, "You need to touch it ONE MORE TIME—REMOVE it", and he laughed. The following Sunday he responded to the evangelistic invitation and really turned his life over to Christ!

THE JESUS VIDEO

One more incident! When asked what I wanted for Christmas the previous year, I had replied, "The Jesus video on DVD in Cantonese and Mandarin languages". Instead the video came in four other languages—English, Spanish, French and Portuguese! Whatever would I do with that! Hmm! There should be Spanish speakers in Panama so I took it along, just in case. Sure enough, my lung specialist in the hospital

dropped hints of spiritual hunger and confusion.
She appeared overwhelmed when I gave her that
Jesus video DVD in those languages. "I speak ALL
those languages," she said, "and my daughters and I
will watch it this coming weekend!" Wow! Surely, it
was no accident that I was put in that hospital! Her
blessing as well as mine!

Vern's back gradually improved to become a
non-issue. He concluded that it was a bruised back
muscle. He stayed faithfully by me in the hospital
except for the trip he took with the team to see the
Panama Canal—one of the original 7 wonders of the
world!

SUMMARY OF RESULTS

Besides the individuals with whom I shared
Jesus, the rest of our team dealt with 124 individuals
about Christ. Among those individuals, 32 were ready
to pray the sinner's prayer for salvation with them!
Only God knows their hearts. I saw this as at least an
initial step, a move toward God in those seeker's lives.
The REAL WORK of follow-up to fulfill
our commission to MAKE DISCIPLES would come
after.

Do not conclude from this report that spiritual
victories came easily there or that results come simply
from the hard work of a great team. Unless the Holy
Spirit prepares and opens hearts, all efforts fall on dry
ground. I observed that spiritual results came in direct

proportion to the prayer support the team brought along. That's why, although I "bombed out" physically, I had plenty of time myself to pray. By keeping in touch daily with prayer partners, my presence on the team was not in vain. (Vern and I also brought the messages in four services).

Chapter 12

CONNECTING THE DOTS

A personal testimony to God's incredible faithfulness in the Orient that spanned over 50 years. (Drawn from notes for a talk which I gave at Covenant Retirement Village of Colorado in August 2009.)

Eccl. 11:1 Cast your bread upon the waters, for after many days you will find it again.

S ometimes we may feel discouraged when we don't see quick results from our service for God or our prayers to Him; but God is faithful. Our feeblest efforts, if done for HIS glory, WILL eventually reap results, sometimes beyond our wildest dreams. We seldom see the whole picture in just a few short years. YOU SEE IT BEST "after many days"—LIKE 50 YEARS!

INTRODUCING A DROPPED PEBBLE

I once read that a pebble dropped into quiet waters will start ripples that will come and go, in and out indefinitely, starting a chain reaction that never ends. Whether or not that is true, it IS true of God's Word. It will NEVER return void. It's just that we don't always live long enough to see it or we lack access to see all the ripples or we don't connect the dots. This time God gave me the chance to see some of the dots connected.

I pray that this simple testimony to God's faithfulness will encourage your heart. It is the story of how God used one very ordinary pebble, dropped in quiet waters, to create an incredible rippling effect. May God use this account to encourage your heart in your areas of service for Him, or in your prayer burdens, or in your outreach to your family—your children or grandchildren. Whenever you share the Father's heart, be assured your efforts will never be in vain.

This story goes back 60 years to 1953 when as a young missionary 23 years old, I arrived in Hong Kong. Refugees were pouring out of China. Sidewalks everywhere were covered with cardboard-box shelters where families of refugees slept. Housing was unavailable. Where would the Mission put me?

One of our senior missionaries had rebuilt a stone house on the small Island of Cheung Chau that was an hour by ferry from the city. During the war, the Japanese had torn it down to use its iron rods for their military forces. Now, that rebuilt missionary's house was to become my first home in Hong Kong. We had no air conditioners back then; but that island boasted an occasional breeze to grant a welcome escape from the tropical heat and humidity of Hong Kong for a tired missionary.

My first job upon arrival was to learn to speak the Cantonese language. This would be my primary task during my first four-year term and part of my second term. It was obvious to me from my Bible school and college days' experience that the language learning side of my brain had never fully developed. My efforts to learn Spanish, Swedish and Greek had been painful. To learn Cantonese, with nine tones and no alphabet, I needed all the help I could get!

As to the location, it really didn't matter where I lived. No language school existed to live near; so I requested to be allowed to live out on that island in that missionary's house. Although thirty thousand Chinese lived there around the water-front, there was no one but my language teacher who could speak English with me! It was an ideal situation for language learning! On the weekends I took a ferry to the city where I attended Chinese church services. I understood nothing from the service, but I could fellowship with other English-speaking missionaries on those weekends. I slept on a camp cot on a missionary's balcony and, oh, how I enjoyed the luxury of English conversation! After nine months of this, the mission found housing for me with a missionary family in the city.

Since Hong Kong was a British colony, English was taught in many schools. In fact some schools were entirely English speaking. With my language study moving so slowly, you will appreciate how glad I was that I didn't need to wait until I was fluent in

Cantonese—like five or ten years down the line, to begin to have SOME kind of ministry.

One of our churches across the harbor on Hong Kong's main island needed someone to fill in for a time to teach an English Sunday School class for high school youth. They requested my help. I jumped at the opportunity although it required an early start on Sunday mornings. I had to take an early bus to the pier. They didn't run often on Sunday mornings. I would wait for a ferry to cross the harbor to take me on the half hour ferry ride and then take a tram car on the other side to the church. About a dozen high school kids attended my class. I faithfully prepared and prayed for those kids and they came very regularly, except for one girl. Chi Ling was exceptionally quiet and usually absent. I needed to visit her to encourage her.

I still remember the English name of the street where she lived--Spring Creek Lane. It was very difficult to find. Of course, I didn't know the streets on that side of the harbor and I didn't have enough Cantonese vocabulary to get directions. Hong Kong's main island downtown consisted of a rim around a mountain, rising fifteen hundred feet from the sea. The island is 2 to 5 miles wide and 15 miles long. Its roads wind like cow paths around the mountain.

Some of Hong Kong's roads are quite unusual with high-risers built against the mountain. I remember years later when my nephew, Jonathan, came by frequent flier miles to Hong Kong to visit me. I took him along downtown on some errands on the main island. We entered a building on a sea level street, took an elevator to the 17th floor and exited out to the 17th floor lobby. There outside the lobby glass doors was a street with a taxi picking up passengers!

As a new missionary, I didn't know the bus routes and I couldn't afford a taxi; so I bought a map, found a bicycle shop and rented a bike so the one-way streets wouldn't matter. (Unfortunately, there were only men's bikes for rent and they were hard to get on.) I biked through the heat and city traffic with my map in hand and eventually found Chi Ling's home to visit her. Yes, she enjoyed the class and would come again. She came once more and then missed a few Sundays. I visited her again and she came again. Her attendance was quite sporadic. It took a few bike trip visits to keep her coming. I shared God's heart for this girl, prayed for her and eventually she trusted Jesus as her Savior!

Many years later Chi Ling told me why she had come to my Sunday School class so spasmodically. It was because she was so poor that she had <u>only one dress</u>. That would be too obvious to all if she came every Sunday and wore the same dress! By coming only occasionally, it would not be so noticeable.

Surely God has a sense of humor. How odd for Him to pick such an unlikely pebble to start unending ripples or chain reactions! One poor high school girl with just one dress! Now what could God do through such a life? *Cast your bread upon the waters, for after many days you will find it again.* That was the promise.

Eventually Chi Ling led her mother and her sister to Christ. In turn her mother's sister, Mrs. Fung, trusted Jesus. I'd like to point out some of the ripples, the chain reactions that came through Chi Ling, her sister, and her aunt, Mrs. Fung. They made themselves available to God and He used them beyond measure. These three pebbles caused ripples fifty some years ago that are still abundantly visible today. The invitation as given in Psalms 66:5 applies here. *"Come and see what God has done, how awesome His works on man's behalf."*

MISSION VISION

In time both Chi Ling and her sister felt God's call to serve Him full-time. They both completed seminary and went into full-time Christian service. Chi Ling went on to serve on the staff of the local Hebron Christian and Missionary Alliance Church. Besides all the lives she touched within that church, she had a deep passion for missions. One day she shared with me her mission vision for her church. It was not just to send out missionaries from her church to far-flung mission fields. She envisioned her church becoming a mission *sending agency* that would send many missionaries globally!! Her church would function as a mission board for many churches to send missionaries around the world! I discouraged her. That was too specialized a job for a single church where the staff would be too busy with local ministries to give the time needed to manage overseas work in a variety of languages and cultures. Fortunately, she didn't follow my advice. Her church became known throughout Hong Kong as a prominent mission sending agency that sent missionaries to touch lives in countries far and near. Only Eternity will tell the world the full impact of just this one phase of Chi Ling's life and ministry! God chose to use one quiet high school girl who had only one dress! One pebble that caused ripples around the world—ripples that last even today! That is just a start to the chain reactions of the ripples from this girl.

CHI LING'S SISTER & PEACE EVANGELICAL CENTERS

Chi Ling's sister married one of her fellow seminary graduates. As a team they planted one church after another in Hong Kong. With a strong emphasis on discipleship, feeding on God's Word and prayer, their "Peace Center" members became effective witnesses for Christ, spawning remarkable church growth. Under the guidance of Chi Ling's sister and brother-in-law, Ng Chu Kwong, the Peace Evangelical Center churches multiplied. The last I heard, they had grown to well over thirty centers in Hong Kong and still growing, even spreading to North America. Their members are known all over Hong Kong as serious Christians whose lives make a difference. These "Peace Evangelical Center churches", as they call themselves, have grown to become almost a denomination themselves in Hong Kong as well as in North America!

Once, after my retirement, I was invited to return to Hong Kong to be their speaker for a 4-day winter conference of the Peace Center churches. There were several hundred key people attending, mostly college youth and young working couples who took vacation time to come apart to rough it in order to seriously study God's Word and its application to their lives. They meant business for God!

The ripples were started by one quiet high school girl who had just one dress, to extend to now over thirty centers scattered all over Hong Kong and abroad. God's incredible faithfulness continues. I chose Chi Ling's story because she was such an ordinary pebble that was so unlikely to send unending ripples. The story doesn't end there.

MRS FUNG'S FLAT

One year I lived on the eleventh floor of an apartment building right across the street from Waterloo Hill. This hill was a partially sawed off mountain which sprouted clusters of upper class high-rise apartment buildings that are twenty to thirty stories high. As I had my Quiet Time on a balcony facing Waterloo Hill's towering buildings, I yearned for even one Bible study to meet in every one of those buildings! Chi Ling's aunt, Mrs. Fung, had a flat in one of those building where she lived. Before Christmas, Mrs. Fung and I planned a Christmas party for the children of her building that would meet in Mrs. Fung's flat. Together, with some of my seminary students, we combed every flat on every floor of her building to invite all the children to her Christmas party. The seminary students helped with the party and Bible story time. Many kids came and loved it. In fact, this developed into a weekly kids' Bible story time in Mrs. Fung's flat.

I wrote to our missionaries, the Don Carlsons, who were then in the United States on furlough. I suggested that, when they returned, they should try to find housing on Waterloo Hill to start home Bible studies among those buildings. They did and, with Mrs. Fung, they contacted the mothers of the children coming weekly to her kids' group. Not surprisingly, this became an evangelistic Bible study for women. In time, a few mothers trusted Christ! What about their husbands? When could THEY be free to come? A lot of prayer went into this. The men replied that their only free time was nine thirty on Sunday mornings! Now these were successful business men who would fly back and forth to the United States on business. They had reached their goals of education, success, wealth and position; yet something was MISSING in their lives. They felt empty. They lived in a spiritual vacuum.

The YWCA owned several whole floors in that same building that housed Mrs. Fung's flat and she was on the board of the YWCA. She easily gained permission to borrow the YWCA's beautiful chapel on Sunday mornings at 9:30 for church services. First a few, then more fathers and mothers came with their children. Special classes were arranged for the children. They had to borrow more rooms on that floor from the Y.

In time they hired a young preacher, So Wing Yui, to help reach these families. In order to contact student-age youth, the preacher got himself hired as a teacher by the Baptist College to teach a course on The Art of Living! He was a favorite teacher. His classes discussed philosophy and the meaning of life. He invited his students to his Waterloo Hill flat on Saturday nights where he and his wife would stir up fried rice and a simple dish to go with it. He reported that up to fifty college kids were coming, sitting around on the floor of his flat, eating from paper plates and having bull sessions on spiritual topics. Some trusted Christ. He invited them to try their Sunday morning worship service at the Y chapel. When the students finally did come, they came en masse, filling the chapel. This whole thing mushroomed. Pastor So started Friday night Bible studies at a rented facility near the Y. Pastor So himself taught one evangelistic Bible study for non-Christians. When class members trusted Christ, they were promoted to discipleship classes taught by others to make room for more non-Christians in the Evangelistic Bible study. More space was rented. Eventually, over a hundred young couples were coming regularly for Friday night Bible studies.

In 1976 they organized to officially become Woh Fook or Blessings Hill Church. This church, being less traditional, attracted talented young Chinese graduates who had studied overseas, found Christ and returned to Hong Kong, but culture-wise, no longer fit well in the traditional Hong Kong churches.

To accommodate their growing numbers, this Waterloo Hill church, known as "Woh Fook" rented a nearby school for Sunday morning services. This was to develop into their first daughter church. Their own church today in 2013 has 1,500 in their Sunday services. They have planted ten daughter churches which in turn have started six more "granddaughter" churches. Since some of these have become mega churches, the total attendance today in Woh Fook's offspring churches exceeds 23,000.

One of their daughter churches bought property and built their own church building, nineteen stories high, which includes space for their own church Bible school! Where land is expensive, you build high instead of wide.

Yan Fook Church also has a significant ministry inside mainland China, including access to printing presses there. Their senior pastor, a converted Communist and trained at Dallas Seminary, has authored many books and pamphlets that are ideal for China's audience and culture. Active laymen from this church enter China with a cell phone and notebook computer. They phone back, "send such and such a book to my cell phone and computer" and in this way relevant material is published and distributed inside mainland China! Only God knows the full outreach through that one church. A very ordinary pebble was available, dropped into quiet waters. Endless ripples continue from a poor high school girl with only one dress!

Cast your bread upon the waters and after many days . . . Wow!

OVERFLOW TO AMERICA

After my retirement in 1997, I was invited by Mrs. Fung to come to Ithaca, New York for a week to speak at home meetings plus a Sunday service to a Chinese congregation. Here's the story behind that outreach. Mrs. Fung had a son who was attending the prestigious Cornell University there. She rented a flat to live nearby and spent her days at the University, visiting with the Chinese students there, befriending them and chatting with them in the lounge, the dining room, the library or the ladies room. She loved those lonely Chinese students so far away from home. She counseled them and became a sort of a surrogate mother to them. She found a retired Chinese pastor running a rice shop in China Town and roped him into leading a Friday night Chinese Bible study for those Chinese students. Eventually Chi Ling's aunt, Mrs. Fung, rented a hall for Sunday services. She got some key Chinese adult believers involved and they organized a Chinese church. During the weekend that I was there, the hall was packed beyond its legal limits. On week nights we met in homes and there were salvation decisions. The Chinese believers began looking to buy a beautiful old church building with a dying congregation that had just a few old seniors left. They have since bought that church which was fully equipped with sound system, organ, piano, and a church library! Now the church is flourishing in that building and is in the process of buying an adjacent building for additional classrooms! God is continuing the ripples with chain reactions from one high school girl with just one dress!

RIPPLES INTO MONGOLIA

When the German Mongol Mission pulled out of Inner Mongolia, we lost our contacts for distributing the colloquial Mongolian Scriptures that we had printed in Hong Kong. For two years, these Scriptures sat in storage in Hong Kong. There sat ten thousand copies of the colloquial Mongolian New Testament, plus nine thousand copies of Genesis and Psalms. What a waste! This was heavy on our hearts. I had shared this burden at Covenant Retirement Village vesper services and two dear ladies there took this need on as a personal prayer burden. Occasionally they would ask me, "Has there been a breakthrough yet? Have those Mongolian Scriptures moved into Inner Mongolia?" I had to answer, "Not yet."

Actually, I still had contacts in Inner Mongolia with Chinese Christians who had known my father. However, the Chinese had little contact with the Mongols. The cities were so filled with Chinese, only Mandarin speaking Mongols could survive there. There was little contact between the two cultures. Whether we would ship by train or truck the thousands of copies of the Mongolian Scriptures, who would dare to receive and store them in that Communist controlled country for who knows how long?

But God was answering prayer. He brought to Inner Mongolia a retired American school teacher (name withheld for security reasons) with a passion to distribute Chinese Bibles. He hired English speaking teachers to run a couple of schools that taught English. In this way he established an answer for being there. He hired couriers who helped him to distribute bi-lingual Chinese-English New Testaments. He built good relationships with local government authorities and the two Chinese registered churches in his city. (One church met on the 12th floor of a commercial building there!) Working low-key with the right people, his activities were permissible. The government was more concerned about religious activity among autonomous peoples like the Tibetans or Mongols who were more closely watched.

In one city of Inner Mongolia, he found a large Chinese church with a congregation of two thousand Chinese and one thousand Mongols! A Christian Mongolian lady, who knew Mandarin, had been, interpreting the Chinese pastor's messages. Here were a thousand Mongolian believers with no Bible that they could read. When he heard of the Mongolian Scriptures waiting in Hong Kong, he then had the contacts to distribute them! All those Mongolian Scriptures were moved to eager hands in Inner Mongolia.

One Mongolian New Testament fell into the hands of a Mongol publisher who became a believer through reading it in his heart language. He eagerly offered to print the New Testament himself, locally.

They would be much cheaper than the Hong Kong ones and would be made with cheaper paper. Our American teacher wished for another forty thousand Mongolian New Testaments to distribute!

In January of 2008, I sent out a prayer letter seeking funding through New Life Literature for further printing "in country". In just one month, thirty donors sent six thousand dollars for the cause. The thirty donors were more significant to me than the dollar amount; because now they too, would be burdened to pray for more Bibles for the Mongols.

The American teacher reported that a friend of his had offered an eight thousand U.S. dollars grant toward printing more Mongolian New Testaments locally if someone would match that grant within two weeks!

Knowing God had blessed her financially, I phoned Chi Ling's aunt, Mrs. Fung, with the news of the matching grant. Would she be interested in helping toward that match? She replied, "If he will raise his grant to ten thousand dollars, I will match it!" He did, and we suddenly had $26,000 toward the project! Thousands of copies of the New Testament were printed, stored in various safe places and distributed by both Mongols and Chinese. By not using India paper, they were so large and bulky that we ended up printing thousands more of just the Gospels of Luke and John. We wanted Luke for the life of Christ and John for His teachings. This would print more copies that would be more portable and give enough light to lead a

Mongol to salvation. Funds were also donated to buy a van which is still being used to distribute the Mongolian Scriptures to nomads across the grasslands. News of Mrs. Fung's enthusiastic matching grant encouraged us to buy up the paper needed before its rise in price and inspired donors to give, thus providing many more Mongols with God's Word.

Who would have thought some fifty five years ago, as I biked through Hong Kong's heat and traffic with a map in hand to find a high school girl with just one dress, how God would eventually use that unlikely pebble, dropped into quiet waters, to someday help me fulfill a heavy burden to reach the Mongols of my childhood with God's precious Word in their own heart language! Thank God for His help in connecting the dots.

Eccl. 11:1 Cast your bread upon the waters, for after many days you will find it again.

ABREVIATIONS USED AND MEANINGS

Co.   Company

DVBS   Daily Vacation Bible School

EFC   Evangelical Free Church

KL   Kuala Limpur, capital city of Malaysia

M. Div   Master of Divinity degree

Pa.   Pennsylvania

PJ's   Pajamas

PTL   Praise the Lord

SOS   Distress call letters

SS   Sunday School

St.   Saint

U.S.   United States of America

USA   United States of America

WWII   World War Two

Y   YMCA or Young Men's Christian Association

DATES OF IMPORTANCE

1889 - Birth of Hjalmar Ekblad, father—in Sweden.

1898-1997 - Hong Kong leased to Great Britain by China for 99 years.

1906 - Ekblad came to America.

Early 1900's - Boxer Rebellion.

1917 – Ekblad traveled from Sweden to China across Siberia. He was on the last train before the Russian revolution.

1918 - Ekblad wed to Alma

1925 - Ekblad married to 2nd wife, Selma Nelson (Doris' mother).

1926-1927 - Ekblads returned to United States because of China's political unrest and stayed for five years to regain U.S. citizenship.

1929 - Birth of Paul Ekblad.

1930 – Birth of Doris Ekblad.

1933 - Ekblads return to Inner Mongolia.

1934 - John and Betty Stam martyred.

1933-36 - Children live in Inner Mongolia.

1936 - Mother died. Children come to United States to live with their aunt.

1937 - Start of Japanese War. Furlough after 3rd marriage.

1945 – Fire burned down home in Wisconsin.

1948 – Doris' three month short term summer mission ministry in Kentucky.

1953 - Doris Arrived in Hong Kong as missionary.

1953 - Gunzel's (1st) Mongolian literary revision of the Bible.

1960 – Undulant fever and Home Emergency, Father's heart attack.

1962 – Doris returns to Hong Kong.

1960's - Doris began teaching at Evangel Seminary.

1979 - President Nixon's visit to China. China's Open Policy.

1981 - Home Assignment.

1982 - First Visit to Inner Mongolia.

1987 - Second Visit to Inner Mongolia.

1991 - Third Visit to Inner Mongolia. Outer Mongolia gained independence from Russia, Old Mongolian Scrip re-introduced in schools. Took Trans-Siberian train trip.

1991 - Trip to Thailand, Australia, Singapore.

1997 - British return Hong Kong to China.

1997 - Retirement. Search for Stams' Grave.

2000 - Colloquial translation of the Mongolian New Testament completed.

2001 - Speaking Trip to Hong Kong. Colloquial translation confirmed.

2002 - Another Trip to Hong Kong for fundraising to print New Testament. Engagement to Vern.

2003 - Colloquial Mongolian New Testament Printed. Wedding and Retired to Covenant Village of Colorado.

2007 – Finding distribution of Colloquial Mongolian New Testament breakthrough.

2008 – Colloquial Mongolian New Testament printed and distributed in country.